Mr. Zhao (right) having a dialogue on the "China Model" with the Naisbitts in Beijing (August 29, 2009)

Mr. Zhao (middle) with the Naisbitts in "imperial robes" (August 31, 2009)

An online program interview about China at China Internet Information Center (September 2, 2009)

The coauthors exchanging views with students at Renmin University of China (March 9, 2010)

Mr. Zhao and his family at Mount Wutai, a sacred place for Buddhism in China (August 4, 2007)

Mr. Zhao (third from the right), also a supervisor at Nankai University, with his doctoral candidates majoring in Regional Economics (June 30, 2004)

Mr. Zhao, Dean of the School of Journalism, Renmin University, talking with graduates (June 18, 2007)

Mr. Zhao, spokesperson for the Chinese People's Political Consultative Conference, being interviewed by journalists (March 2, 2010)

Mr. Zhao (right) and Luis Palau, a well-known American religious leader, taking part in the premiere of the English version of *Riverside Talks* (August 31, 2006)

Mr. Zhao (right) and U.N. Secretary-General Kofi Annan attending a national music concert of China entitled "A Chinese Culture Tour to the United States" (August 24, 2000)

Mr. Zhao (right) having an interview with former CBS News anchor Dan Rather in New York (February 21, 2008)

Mr. Zhao (middle) with the 56th U.S. Secretary of State, Henry Kissinger (right), and the 60th U.S. Secretary of State, George Schultz (June 17, 2006).

Mr. Zhao (middle) attending the Fifth Meeting of the China-EU Round Table in Tianjin, China (May 18, 2009)

Mr. Zhao (left) and former Japanese Prime Minister Ryutaro Hashimoto (right) visiting the photo exhibition: "Peace and Friendship, Jointly Create Prosperity — Pictures of Friendship Between Chinese and Japanese" in Tokyo (July 28, 2005)

Doris Naisbitt and John Naisbitt with their children and grandchildren (June 2009)

John Naisbitt at work (February 2009)

The Naisbitts' study (in the spring of 2009)

John Naisbitt (middle) and Doris Naisbitt (right) in front of the special plane of Megatrend University in Belgrade (August 2009)

Doris Naisbitt and John Naisbitt at the Naisbitt China Research Institute in Tianjin (June 2009)

Mr. Naisbitt making a speech at the Frankfurt Book Fair in Germany (October 2009)

The Naisbitts on vacation in Austria (in the summer of 2009)

The Naisbitts having an interview with the media at Tianjin University of Finance and Economics

Mr. Naisbitt with a lama of the Drebung Monastery in Lhasa (September 2009)

The Naisbitts visiting a primary school in Lhasa (September 2009)

Zhao Qizheng
John Naisbitt and Doris Naisbitt

A DIALOGUE BETWEEN EAST AND WEST

THE CHINA MODEL

NEW WORLD PRESS

First Edition 2010

By Zhao Qizheng, John Naisbitt and Doris Naisbitt
Translated by Zhang Hongbin and Xu Jingguo
Edited by Xu Jingguo, Li Shujuan and Ge Wencong
Cover Design by He Yuting

ISBN 978 – 7 – 5104 – 1085 – 7

Published by
NEW WORLD PRESS
24 Baiwanzhuang Street, Beijing 100037, China

Published by
NEW WORLD PRESS
24 Baiwanzhuang Street, Beijing 100037, China
Tel: 86 – 10 – 68995968
Fax: 86 – 10 – 68998705
Website: www. newworld – press. com
E – mail: frank@ nwp. com. cn

Printed in the People's Republic of China

Acknowledgements

We would like to take this opportunity to express our thanks to all those people who have contributed their efforts to the publication of this book. We know it is a complicated process to edit a book like this in both Chinese and English. From the conception to the birth of our brainchild, we received help from many of our friends in various kinds of work, including recording, transcription, editing, translation, and communication. Help and support also came from the New World Press, the Bridge Art Center, and the State Council Information Office of China.

We are particularly grateful to Madame Wu Wei, Deputy Director-General of the State Council Information Office of China, for the initial suggestion of the book and her constant support, without which it would not have been possible to complete this book. We are indebted to Mr. Zhou Mingwei, President of China International Publishing Group, and Mr. Huang Youyi, Vice President and concurrently Editor-in-Chief of China International Publishing Group, for contribution of their bright ideas about the topic design for the book.

Many thanks go to Mr. Zhu Yinghuang, former Editor-in-Chief of *China Daily*, and Dr. Paul Adams, visiting professor of Foreign Languages at Tsinghua University, for polishing and reviewing the English version of the book. Thanks also go to Mr. Zhang Hongbin, Senior Interpreter of the State Council Information Office, for excellent onsite interpretation to facilitate the dialogue between the coauthors; to Ms. Zhong Zhenfen for the structural design and editing of the Chinese version of the book; to Ms. Zhang Haihua and Dr. Xu Jingguo for help with coordination and communication in the process of book publication; and to Dr. Liang Tingting and Dr. Wang Gengxi for proofreading the dialogue part of the book.

We greatly appreciate the kindness and generosity of the Bridge Art Center for providing and decorating the venue for the dialogue. And we are greatly obliged to Madame Zhang Hai'ou, Deputy Editor-in-Chief of the New World Press, and the editorial staff under her direction for their outstanding work and painstaking efforts in the successful publication of the book.

Zhao Qizheng
Doris Naisbitt
John Naisbitt

Preface I

By Zhao Qizheng

I came to know about John Naisbitt through *Megatrends* in the early 1980s. As late as 2000, I had the honor to meet with John and his very talented wife, Doris, in Beijing. In May 2009, when they wrote *China's Megatrends*, they told me their conception of writing about "the eight pillars of the new society of China" and sincerely invited me to give them my opinion. As an American and a European (Doris is a German-speaking Austrian), John and Doris extracted "the eight pillars" from quantities of chaotic and contradicting data about China. This not only surprised me, but also made me admire them. If my opinion were given in a twinkling, it would be crude and rash, and I was afraid it might contain my Chinese viewpoint and affect their (non-Chinese) way of expression. Therefore, I told them that Chinese could understand "the eight pillars," which were also in agreement with the facts of carrying out the reform and opening-up policies over the previous 30 years, and the facts were the basis of their writing—to be more precise, their research in the field of social science.

The concepts, policies, practices and achievements in the past 30 years since China started the reform and opening up have been summarized and called the "China Road," the "China Model" or the "China Case." However, there are great differences in the descriptions of China in various media of the world. The Western media say that there are different prospects for China at the crossroads: An immature China, a chaotic China, or an economically strong but arrogant China. The observation of the same China has come to a conclusion of a multiform China.

Doris, John and I have discussed the difficulty and method of observing China. We hold that China is like a rapidly moving train, not only with many carriages—more than 30 provinces and municipalities—but also with many passengers, 1. 3 billion people of 56 ethnic groups. If one stands at the roadside or even 10 thousand miles away to observe the train, one cannot clearly see the exterior of the train on the move, let alone its interior; hence, this is unavoidably an inaccurate description, not to mention a fairly correct comment. Doris and John are among a few Western writers on the China train for investigations (Another writer who has left a deep impression on Chinese is Dr. Robert Laurence Kuhn, who has provided a new perspective by proposing four guiding principles for China's reform).

In our dialogue, the three of us discussed such an issue: Because it is difficult to observe China even on the China train in the face of imbalanced development of 34 provinces and municipalities, unequal distribution of wealth among 1. 3 billion people, and geo-cultural variations in regions, what on earth would be the method for understanding the essence of China?

Doris asked me a question bordering on philosophy (I have always held that people whose mother tongue is German are often good at philosophical thinking): Whether a description of China's social system could be as concise as that of the Western social system. I acknowledged that more words would be needed to describe China's social system, and my reason was that the explanation of China has to be comparatively long because it has been only 60 years since the establishment of China's socialist system and even only 30 years since the start of the reform and opening up, whereas the Western social system has a history of almost 200 years. However, I believe that when China affairs are more familiar to the world in another 30 to 50 years, it will be possible to use a relatively simple expression as expected by Doris to describe China. I also believe that the railway for the China train is one for peaceful development and China will make contributions to global harmony in the process of building a harmonious society.

In our in-depth discussions, I expressed my view that although China has made great progress that attracts worldwide attention in a relatively short period of time, the "China Model" is still in the present continuous tense. At present China is at the initial stage of socialism with Chinese characteristics, and it needs to be improved in the continuous long-term practice. People need to notice that there are many different, even greatly disparate definitions and interpretations of the "China Model" in the world, and there exists no consensus of the same kind. Some developing countries are willing to study such a "case," namely, "the practical process" of Chinese development, and learn something from practices in China's reform and opening up, just as China would like to learn from some practices of other countries in social and economic development. This is a natural phenomenon against the backdrop of globalization. China has no intention to export its "model," because it is against the philosophy that China has constantly insisted on, that is, the formulation of policies by a given country must be combined with its own conditions. China should follow this approach, so should other developing countries.

I very much cherish the opportunity of having a dialogue among the three of us. I have learned a lot from the cross-lingual and cross-cultural exchanges in a most frank way during these five meetings, each for half of the day. It would be our honor if the readers at home and abroad can get some help in their understanding of China from this concise book.

Preface II

By Doris Naisbitt and John Naisbitt

Our first big trip together was made to China in 2000. One of the highlights was our invitation to meet with Mr. Zhao Qizheng, Minister of Information Office of the State Council of China. It was a very nice meeting with several vice ministers in attendance. All was going well with a general discussion about telling China's story to the world and lamenting the widespread ignorance in the West about what was really going on in China. The meeting was the beginning of a strong friendship with Minister Zhao for us.

Ten years later we met again and talked about the changes we had witnessed and in which Mr. Zhao had participated and how much China had achieved in those years. But we also talked about China's shortcomings, its problems and challenges. And, last but not least, about how little the real China is known in the West. Thus the idea of this dialogue was born, and we were happy to agree to an open, unlimited discussion about China's past, present and future.

The above is the cause for the coming out of the book before you. But to begin with, we'd like to say a few words about the historical context that we brought to the dialogue.

More than 200 years ago the United States of America laid the foundation for a modern democracy. Over time the American system became the model for most countries of the so-called West. This new social/economic model, which combined democracy and capitalism, helped the West to surge ahead, leaving India and China, which until the 1800s had made up 50 percent of the global gross domestic product, way behind.

At the beginning of the 20th century another model seemed to be on the rise: Marx and Engels' theory of a classless society was implemented in the Soviet Union as a diametrical alternative to the Western democratic model. Communism should become the socialist alternative to capitalism and, as with the American model, some other countries followed the Communist Soviet model. The rest is history. The Soviet Union fell apart and many communist states made a U-turn and embraced Western democracy and capitalism.

In the face of the impracticality of a classless society and the fall of the Soviet Union, America and Europe became the conductors of the global economy, and America the only remaining superpower. The values of the West were declared the ultimate and universal mold for any nation which claimed a share in shaping the 21st century.

In the first decade of the new century and in the foreboding of a serious crisis in the West, China's ability to sustain economic growth slowly caught the attention of the former dominating nations of the world by China's creating its own model: A new social economic system, which we call "Vertical Democracy."

Not many people in the West associate the word "democracy" with China. But even Western democracies would not match the criteria of the ancient Greek model for democracy. For the Greeks, democracy was literally (*demos*—people, and *kratia*—reign) meaning "reign of the people."

Over the centuries since ancient Greece we have seen that the "reign of the people" can be created in many different ways. Picture any Western-style democracy today, where the justification for governing is winning an election. To win, one party used to try to prove it would be better at governing than another party. But unfortunately in many countries, and particularly in the United States today, it seems increasingly like the formula for success is not to present a better answer, but to make the other side look as unfit to govern as possible. Instead of working together on common goals, hostility and gridlock increasingly dominate the Western political landscape and seem to make it daily more ineffective.

Here in China the "reign of the people" is a work in progress. Its beginning little more than 30 years ago was a dramatic U-turn: Mao's ideological utopianism was replaced by Deng Xiaoping's pragmatic realism.

In our understanding, the first step in the process was Deng's call for the "emancipation of the mind." What has evolved since then is a political structure based on the dynamic interplay between top-down and bottom-up forces. Many in the West find it difficult to believe that any form of democracy could exist in China because there is not a great deal of awareness about the bottom-up forces and the increasing power these forces have within the system, a phenomenon we have discussed with Minister Zhao in this dialogue.

Deng started China's policy of trial and error on huge scale, encouraging entrepreneurship, creating Special Economic Zones, and witnessing successful private enterprises replacing moribund state-owned enterprises. Foreign capital started to flow into the country, at first under the eyes of the central government, then loosening up slowly until recently, in 2009, the long-time, bottom-up practice of provinces and companies dealing directly with foreign countries and companies without going through Beijing was codified by the central government. Today 70 percent of the Chinese economy is in the private sector, a condition the West seems to be totally unaware of.

Despite embracing a market economy, the Chinese leadership is still wearing the communist coat, and the Communist Party of China holds on to its command and control in governing the country—but the concept of what command and control mean has changed radically over the last 30 years. The party has changed from an arbitrary top-down autocracy to a functioning one-party leadership with strong bottom-up participation, a vertically organized democratic society with increasing transparency in making and carrying out decisions, something Minister Zhao and we emphasize.

For two years, we have had 28 researchers at the Naisbitt China Institute at Tianjin University of Finance and Economics and Nankai University working to replicate the local newspaper monitoring project conducted in the United States in the early 1980s which led to the publication of *Megatrends* in 1982. This research has discovered an extremely active intellectual, artistic, political and social life throughout China, which is freely reported in the local press. Local newspapers are becoming forums for reporting the best ideas to improve the quality of people's life in China and also to root out corruption and those forces which may be working against the common good.

"Crossing the river by feeling for the stones" has become China's strategy. In this process, the central government announces a new initiative and encourages competitive experimentation at all levels of government and the private sector. Provincial governors and local mayors, as well as private sector entrepreneurs, all compete to develop the latest ideas regarding energy efficiency, new market development, social processes, healthcare or whatever might contribute to China's development. The central government monitors success, and when this is identified, develops a policy for the country. This top-down, bottom-up process is increasingly applied not only to economic issues, but also to social, cultural and even political spheres of life. Economic and political structures have changed and people are beginning to enjoy a level of social and individual experimentation and freedom that they have never experienced before in China's history. They are defining their own roles and their own contributions.

China's top-down, bottom-up model of a vertical democracy began in the economic sphere, but we have seen how it now applies to judicial reform, social and economic developments, social welfare system, healthcare, artistic expression, architecture and many other areas of daily life. In this continuing democratization process, elections of village leaders are now held in 800,000 villages in China. During our last visit in Tibet we asked an old farmer how they got their village leader. "We choose him," he said. "And how?" we asked. "Like this," he said, gesturing putting a ballot in a voting box. "What if he does a lousy job?" "Then we kick him out and try No. 2," he said with a grin.

In 1981 a group of Western economists in China predicted that it would take China at least a hundred years to climb out of poverty. Thirty years later China has become the second largest economy in the world. The result the Chinese leadership has achieved in its own way has led to an approval rating of 89 percent by the "reign of the people" (according to the Pew Center, the American polling group). This figure is not matched in any other democracy the Pew Center has surveyed. And despite all the bumps in the road, China is benefitting from diversity while sustaining order and harmony.

China is shaping a vertical democracy based on its own history, values and needs. To what degree it will match Western perceptions troubles only the West. Minister Zhao and we totally agree that China has its own goals and dreams. How to get there its people will decide.

Part One: About the "China Model"

Part Two: On the Global Understanding of China

Part Three: How to Tell China's Story Better

Part Four: On Science, Education and Intellectual Property

Part Five: Where Will China Go?

About the "China Model"

Zhao Qizheng ("**Zhao**" **hereafter**) : Glad to meet you once again in Beijing, and my warmest congratulations on the publication of both the Chinese and German versions of your new book, *China's Megatrends*. ①

The Naisbitts: Thank you!

Zhao: After reading your new book, one issue came to mind. You have provided insight into China after coming to China for more than four decades and doing lots of studies and up-to-date research by the staff of your institute in China. And, not to forget, you have done so also by using your rather unique analytic approach. Now, media in all parts of the world are talking about China every day. However, most of these media people have not put in as much work as you have in your study of China. Many of their opinions on China are superficial and confusing, and even misleading to readers.

John Naisbitt ("**John**" **hereafter**) : Yes, it's true. In a way we all build our opinions on what we believe is right or wrong. So we should not be surprised that many Western journalists are judging China against their own opinions and biases and against Western history and Western culture. It is a view from the outside, not an inside view of China. Our research on China's megatrends did not have a set direction. During our research, 28 staff of the Naisbitt China Institute monitored more than 100 local newspapers from all over China. We needed to know what was really happening on the ground. We wanted

---

① John Naisbitt and Doris Naisbitt, *China's Megatrends* (Jilin Publishing Group, China Industry & Commerce Associated Press Co. Ltd, September 2009; Hanser, September 2009; Harper Business, January 2010).

to know what was in the minds of the Chinese people. What are their hopes, dreams and complaints?

Zhao: We wish that the reports would conform more to reality. As for editorials and commentaries, they are shaped by the viewpoints of individual media organizations.

Doris Naisbitt ("**Doris**" **hereafter**): And the West wants China to be more open and accept more freedom in reporting about China.

Zhao: There are some trans-cultural and trans-ideological difficulties for Western reporters in understanding the opening up and freedom in China. However, they should be able to notice that their work conditions have been improving year by year.

John: That's it. As said before, each side starts from its own point of view. China cannot change what Western journalists write about China. But China can improve its own dealings with Western media.

Zhao: From our side, we also encounter cultural differences when dealing with Western media. Your penetrating observation of China is really commendable, together with your meticulous research method and positive attitude. What kind of responses do you expect to your new book?

John: We expect *China's Megatrends* to draw public attention. The West thinks that China can only be sustainable if it adopts Western democracy. This is their starting basis. How well does China fit Western values and standards? The story we tell about China has not been heard before. And we should not be surprised if the West will not embrace it.

Zhao: I would expect that those Western readers who want to understand China will welcome your book and would, more or less, agree with its viewpoint. But there will be some people in political and media circles who will not accept such views. It is not easy to change one's habitual way of thinking.

Driving in the right direction

Doris: I think that we will face two kinds of responses. One is the very good response that we got recently in Finland. After being interviewed, one journalist said to us, "How come I didn't know that? How come I haven't heard all of that? How come that nobody said that before you did?" So, that is the positive side. The other side will be quite different. John and I think that it will be more like a joke that is quite common in Austria. The joke goes: A driver is approaching a superhighway. He enters the highway, and after driving for a little while, the radio announces a warning: "Superhighway West #4 direction of Vienna, a ghost driver warning."

John: A ghost driver is a driver who drives against traffic.

Doris: Yes. So the radio shouts: "A ghost driver is on the highway. Be careful!" The driver looks stricken: "What are they talking about? There are hundreds of ghost drivers coming at me!" In the metaphor, applied to reporting about China, we are seen as the ghost drivers, driving against the traffic. But we, of course, believe we are driving in the right direction. Some journalists have already warned us that we might crash.

Zhao: That very German-style metaphor of yours tells people that sometimes seemingly correct customs or even routine regulations are in fact not correct. If we look back in history, we find that many people who took the lead in telling the truth were in the minority; sometimes the truth is in the hands of the minority. The Polish astronomer Copernicus, who first put forward the theory that the Earth revolves around the Sun, represented the minority. In the beginning of the last century, when Albert Einstein put forward his theory of relativity, many physicists disagreed with him. But in the end he was the victorious minority. Therefore, the minority might be closer to the truth.

Due to the support of data coming from experiments or calculations, the truth of science can be acknowledged rather quickly. However, views in social science, especially in ideology, take a relatively long time for people to accept. So bravery and perseverance are required on the part of those who have put forward the truth.

Doris: Also, we are not only dealing with questioning facts. The discussion is quite emotional. And it is very hard to argue against emotions with rational facts. Emotions often override facts.

John: There's another consideration in telling China's story. The West does not want to hear it. It does not fit the picture that is burned into Western thinking. The West resents China coming up so fast against the great West, looking as good as the West itself. This is where the emotions come in. People in the West get very emotional that maybe China is replacing the West as the most important power in the world.

Zhao: Some Western powers in history and even today have bullied other countries during and after their rise. If they look at China from these experiences, they will naturally feel not at ease, or even get agitated at the development of China.

China in the eyes of Western entrepreneurs

Zhao: I believe any country's development is due to the great efforts made by its government and people, to the correct policies it implements, to its rich resources and to the full play of its people's wisdom and diligence. However, in today's economic globalization, external conditions also become a necessary factor for consideration in the development of a country. Both the outer world and China are external conditions to each other in a reciprocal relationship. Therefore, it is China's wish that the world make fair judgments about its development. If they are too emotional or always proceed from ideology in judging China, they will come to conclusions, which do not reflect reality and this will not be good for them. Therefore, understanding China is not only what the Chinese people wish for, but also a reasonable attitude required of all sober-minded people.

John: In general, entrepreneurs and the corporate world are much more receptive to information about China; they want and need to know more about China. Businessmen are willing to listen to China's real story. But people in general, whether it is the West or the East, have their own problems, their own local economic considerations, plans and hopes. So it's often hard to get them interested in the bigger picture.

Zhao: Generally speaking, Western entrepreneurs are more objective than politicians in observing China, because they have to ascertain

China's investment environment and calculate their input and output when they want to cooperate economically with China. If their judgment is not objective, their enterprises will fail in the Chinese market. No wonder, when there are hearings about China issues on Capitol Hill, often the opinions of the entrepreneurs are more practical and reasonable. For example, several years ago, when the U. S. Congress discussed whether to give the Most Favored Nation (MFN) status to China, nearly all the American top 500 companies listed in *Fortune* magazine were in favor of granting it to China, and they gave their reasons. Their opinions did play a role at the hearings.

In addition to what you have said just now—that some people in the West have worries about what kind of role China will play after its rise as a great power in the world—they also have various incorrect notions. In fact, it is not easy to observe China because it is too large a country undergoing too rapid changes. China is like a fast-moving train, and one must drive in a car at the same speed—just like you two, so that one is able to see more clearly what this China train is really like. If one only stands there to observe China, even with a telescope, one can never get a correct picture.

Balancing between speed and stability

Doris: Yes. But let me ask you a pointed question. Just now you mentioned that China is developing very fast. As a Westerner, I would say, "Yes, China is driving at such high speed that it exceeds the speed limit. So, China has to slow down."

Zhao: Over the past few years, we have also been thinking about this issue of whether we need to keep the annual GDP growth at or even above 10 percent. We feel the need to slow down a little bit and control the speed a little bit so as to more comprehensively and carefully deal with such issues as the imbalances of national economy and people's livelihood, cultural development and environmental protection. This is in line with the concept of "Scientific Outlook on Development" proposed by Chinese leader Hu Jintao. It also means we should pay attention not only to the growth rate of the gross domestic product, but also to the progress of society as a whole and to the sustainability of development.

John: Let me just say that there is a delicate balance here, because we know that maintaining stability is so important to China. To maintain stability, there must be continuous growth at some level, maybe not 10 percent, but near that figure. But what you said has to be the balance with the understanding that to continue the stability of the country, there must be a certain measure of continuous growth. In short, a delicate balance should be kept between growth and stability.

Zhao: That is a real challenge for the Communist Party of China and the Chinese government.

In recent years, people in China have been discussing two issues: One is how to keep an appropriate growth rate for sustainable development and the other is how to raise people's consciousness of cultural development while maintaining an appropriate economic growth rate. In other words, we need to see synchronized progress in both economy and culture. Going too fast may lead to the neglect of cultural development. This is many people's concern in China today.

I once told some Chinese university students: "When you run a 100-meter dash in the field, you may take off some clothes and run as fast as you can. But after you finish running, you need to come back and put on your clothes. " The students understood what I meant was that culture was what we needed. China's construction needs many years' efforts, and it should be like running a marathon. To run a marathon with the speed of a 100-meter dash is certainly not appropriate. Thus, China needs to adjust its economic growth rate to an appropriate level for sustainable development.

Extending help to Western journalists

John: The purpose of our discussion is also to overcome prejudice or misunderstanding on both sides. If we pick up our ghost driver and the train exceeding the speed limit, the standpoint of the West is that it took it 500 years to create traffic rules that benefit the participants in the traffic. The West had the Renaissance, the Enlightenment, the French Revolution and finally America as a model for modern democracy. So, the West says, " We have, by now, formed the perfect and ultimate system. " And you remember Francis Fukuyama's[1] book *The End of History and the Last Man*, where he writes that " What we may be witnessing is ... the endpoint of mankind's ideological evolution and the universalization of Western liberal democracy as the final form of human government. " Anybody who wants to try the sort of speed in a one-eye level of the West has to move to that Western pattern of running traffic rules.

Now this, in our opinion, does not have to be right. In fact, what we

---

[1] Francis Fukuyama is an American-Japanese scholar, consultant to the Rand Corporation and professor of international political economy at the Johns Hopkins University School of Advanced International Studies. His works include *The End of History and the Last Man* (Free Press, 1992); *Trust: The Social Virtues and the Creation of Prosperity* (Free Press, 1995); and *The Great Disruption: Human Nature and the Reconstruction of Social Order* (Free Press, 1999).

have found is that China is creating a whole new system. The traffic rules that serve the people in China are much better than any Western traffic rules that would serve this country. But there are two sides of looking at something. China has the duty or the responsibility to deliver all the information, comprehensive and timely information, to Western journalists. We are mostly talking about the picture painted by journalists. The Western journalists, on the other hand, have the responsibility to collect all the information comprehensively and in time to pass it on to their readers. We have been saying there is a gap on both sides. On the one hand, China has failed to give the information or have all the information accessible. At least, that is the way it is perceived in the West. And on the other hand the West does not do a good job in really reporting the facts and being objective in its reporting.

Zhao: I've read the Fukuyama book you mentioned, but I disagree with his viewpoint. Just this week, Professor Fukuyama told Japanese journalists that the unexpectedly rapid development of the Chinese economy has demonstrated the validity of China's model. He believes that it is unlikely for China to wholly copy Western concepts in its development of democracy and its legal system. Instead, China will most probably adopt an approach that emphasizes people's livelihood in a practical and gradual style. It will try to solve such issues as environment protection, land taken for development, and corruption cases among local officials in a gradual way, thus updating the system through interactions between government and people. He also made an important remark in the sense that "the end of history" still needs further deliberation and improvement and that a place should be reserved for China in the treasure-house of human ideology. ①

---

① See the interview with Fukuyama "Japan should face the century of China" in *Chuokoron* (Central Review in Japanese) September issue, 2009.

Doris: We could not agree more with what Professor Fukuyama has said recently to modify his own view on the end of history. In fact, as you know, the whole book of *China's Megatrends* is dedicated to China's new model. As soon as we were sure that China was not only changing within a system, but creating a whole new social/economic model, analyzing this model became a core question of the book. Shall we describe it?

Zhao: It's a good idea. There are different China perspectives in today's world. For example, the so-called "Beijing Consensus"① is one perspective on China. Other views on the "China Model" represent different China perspectives.

Understanding the "China Model"

John: People found this and that model for China; I have not heard a single satisfying description. What do people say? What does China say? I don't think China has ever explained its model other than "socialism with Chinese characteristics." But that doesn't explain anything. What is socialism with Chinese characteristics?

Doris: I would add that if you would ask me or John what the model or the political system of Europe or the U. S. is, we will give you a clear answer: It's a democracy. If we ask you how you would characterize the Chinese system, and you would not paraphrase its

---

① In May 2004 Joshua Cooper Ramo, a senior consultant for Goldman Sachs, made a speech under the title "The Beijing Consensus" in London. His speech was then published on the website of the Foreign Policy Center, a famous British think tank, and soon strongly resonated among Europe, China and other countries of the world. The economic miracle of China and the "China Model" behind it became the focus of the world attention for a while.

characteristics, but give it a name, what would that name be? What form of government does China have?

Zhao: Well, I think the Chinese themselves have not used words like the "China Model" because the word "model" in English has several implications, with one meaning "example to follow." The reason Chinese do not use this word is to avoid the implication of becoming an example to be followed by others. If we really need to give a definition of "China Model," it can be defined as a summary of concepts, policies, strategies and practices as well as problems that have arisen over the past six decades, particularly the past three decades of building socialism with Chinese characteristics. Perhaps it is more appropriate to call it "China Case." It is still under way, in the present continuous tense.

Maybe I can explain some features of China's system in relatively simple terms. First, the concept is that the government is for the people, and guides the people forward in economic, cultural, scientific and technological advancement; and the ruling party should represent the fundamental interests of the broadest masses of the people. Second, the country's development proceeds from people's needs, and adheres to a comprehensive, coordinated and sustainable path, which is called the "Scientific Outlook on Development." Third, in practice, a prudent approach is combined with bold experiments, and all the major reforms are first tried in certain areas before they are popularized. For example, the local government of Shanghai's Pudong New Area, where I once worked, conducted many pilot projects before its experiences were introduced to other parts of the country.

John: I'm very puzzled. I'm puzzled because you say you have socialism with Chinese characteristics. Market economy is not socialism, so I'm puzzled. I don't understand what's the real emphasis here. Is it "market economy"? Or is it "Chinese characteristics"? But socialism is not market economy, as one understands classical socialism.

Zhao: According to the traditional view, socialism is really thought to be incompatible with market economy to some extent; therefore, Deng Xiaoping said, "The proportion of planning to market forces is not the essential difference between socialism and capitalism. A planned economy is not equivalent to socialism, because there is planning under capitalism, too; a market economy is not capitalism, because there are markets under socialism, too. Planning and market forces are both means for controlling economic activity."[1] It is Deng's great creation, and it has been realized in China.

Doris: With all due respect, you're beating around the bush. The question was: How would you, with one or two words, describe the political system of China? Your answer was a very long list of things.

Zhao: The system of socialism with Chinese characteristics came into being about 30 years ago. It is a newly emerging thing, and the world may not be able to fully understand it. Therefore, detailed explanations are necessary. The Western system has a history of more than 200 years, and people are very familiar with it. Naturally, a simple description of it is enough for understanding.

Doris: Maybe the question was not clear. So let me put it this way:

---

① *Selected Works of Deng Xiaoping* (Beijing: Foreign Languages Press), 1994, Vol. 3 (1982-1992), 361.

"What's the name for the relationship between John and me?" Would you say, "Well, John and Doris are having very nice meals together; Doris is cooking and John's washing the dishes; they work very well together; they create a very nice home, share the similar interests and work on the same goals?" That will give you an explanation of characteristics of our relationship. But the answer is one word: John and Doris are "married." They are a couple.

John: We are in love (laughing).

Doris: Don't distract! I repeat the question: What form of government does China have? Could you please characterize the relationship in one word between the Chinese people and government?

Zhao: In Chinese "*guojia*" (country) is a compound word of "*guo*" (state) combined with "*jia*" (family), with "*guo*" implying a big family. Local government officials in the feudal society for several thousand years were called "*fumu guan*" (parent officials), and officials said that they loved their subjects like their own children, but actually the relationship between the government and people was one between the ruling and the ruled. Today the ruling party and government set strict demands on themselves that they should use the power only for the people; they should have affection for the people; and they should serve the interests of the people. Meanwhile, the people require that the government continuously advance their interests in economics, politics, and culture, which should be seen in the government's making earnest efforts to do practical work satisfactorily for the people. In this way, the old relationship between the government and the people in the feudal society has been completely reversed. However, we also have problems such as bureaucracy and corruption, which people feel discontented with. We notice the existence of these problems, but we still need to improve our legal system and enhance supervision over the government.

In the process of development, we have encountered numerous difficulties. Because China is a country with a big population and various ethnic groups, and a country with great regional disparities, China's development must be unique. Before 1949, China tried to follow the Western practice, but failed. And then from 1949 to 1959, it mainly followed the Soviet practice, but the living standard of the people was improved very slowly. After 1978, Deng Xiaoping put forward the theory of building socialism with Chinese characteristics. We can say this is a new path that has never been taken by anyone before, and we have made it.

Doris: Did the Western model fail? Or did the execution of the model fail? There's a difference.

Zhao: Well, in other words, the model from outside failed to suit the national conditions of China and was not fit for growth in China.

John: In regard to your answer to Doris' question, we have been talking about China's story. What's China's story to the world? The world needs to understand what China is doing. If you insist on calling it socialism when you have got mostly a market economy, that is very confusing, that is not telling your story. People are confused and don't understand. That's why we do not call it only socialism of some kind. It is not only modifying socialism. China is working on the creation of an entirely new model. It's new governance; it's a new way of doing things. When we were looking for a name to describe that model, we were aware that it is not market economy or socialism. China is walking a new path, and that has to be apparent when China's story is told to the world. As we analyzed the structure, we came to call it "Vertical Democracy." If you keep calling it socialism, then people would not get it at all.

Zhao: Deng Xiaoping has considered this issue and characterized the system with a modifier, that is, "socialism with Chinese characteristics." So it's different from European socialism or Indian socialism. It is a socialism defined by Deng Xiaoping's theory. In other words, you may call it "Deng Xiaoping's socialism."

John: (Laughing) You know, it seems to me if you want the world to understand the new China, you can't use the old vocabulary. The very important thing is when you move into a new paradigm, which you have, you cannot hold on to old vocabulary. How can you describe a new paradigm with old vocabulary?

The old paradigm raises some eyebrows in the West. What could Europeans identify with Chinese characteristics? Communism? Or ideology? Everything more negative than positive. So why not leave your cocoon of communism and be what you are? You are now a butterfly, but you still hide in the cocoon, and you'll say, "We do not want to be a model." Why do you not want to be a model? Why do you say, "We do not want to be a model?" The West is not at all shy in presenting itself as the one and only acceptable model. Europe says it has the Renaissance and the Enlightenment, the ethics, the morals and human rights. But how much did that help Africa, for example? How can Europe be a model for emerging countries?

In business and life, if you are not convinced of yourself, how can you convince anyone else? If you say, "We are not a model," you put your achievements down. So emancipate yourself. Be proud of it.

Don't hide behind the old name because that doesn't represent what you are any more. Come out and celebrate your country.

Zhao: China has already "sinicized" Karl Marx's communism, integrating it into traditional Chinese culture and ideology and incorporating it into the era of economic globalization. China's communism is quite different from the communism once practiced by the former Soviet Union and Eastern European countries. In China, "socialism" and "communism" are not negative words. If we give up the two words, many Chinese will be puzzled and strongly oppose the abandonment. Overseas people may find it difficult to understand the expression "socialism with Chinese characteristics," whereas the overwhelming majority of Chinese not only understand it but also endorse it. When we use the expression, we must first consider its adoption by the Chinese people, then the understanding of people in other countries.

When Europeans and Americans mention "socialism," they associate it with the socialism of the former Soviet Union and Eastern Europe, even with *Gulag Archipelago*① and *Doctor Zhivago*.② But there is no such association when people talk about socialism in China, because there are no such stories in China.

---

① The expression comes from the novel by Alexander Solzhenitsyn, a writer of the former U. S. S. R. , to describe the labor camp life in that country. It is a metonymy in which the writer compares the U. S. S. R. to an ocean with islands of prisons and labor camps. He calls them an archipelago. The writer was awarded the Nobel Prize in Literature in 1970.

② A novel by Boris Pasternak, a famous poet and novelist of the former U. S. S. R. The story tells the tragic life of Dr. Zhivago against the historical background of World War I and the Pre- and Post-October Revolution, reflecting the perplexity of a generation of intellectuals in the October Revolution and enabling the reader to understand from one aspect some cruel reality of society during the period of the Russian civil war. The author was awarded the Nobel Prize in Literature in 1958.

Presenting a completely new China

Doris: I do not believe there are only negative examples of what happened in communist regimes in the West. I also think China has its negative cases during communism. Examples of negative consequences of communism cannot only be found in Eastern Europe. China went through a lot of setbacks before its reform and opening up to the outside world. Even with the biggest sympathy for China, under the banner of communism not only good things happened here in China.

But what took place in the past cannot be changed. We are here to talk about the future, which we can form. Communism is connected with Marx, and I am by far not a specialist on Karl Marx. However, if you only look at the main features of Karl Marx, the dream was to create a classless society and do away with the social distinction between proletariat and the bourgeoisie. Now, if you have a market economy, it is impossible to have classless society.

Despite all ideological thinking, people dream different dreams. That was the first great achievement of the new China, to allow people to have their own dreams. One person dreams of economic success and another of spiritual fulfillment. The measurement of success for the world today is, to a certain degree, economic success. You never have a capitalist society in a Marxist system, whatever romantic side you might read into it. So by definition whether we call it communism or Marxism, there is a problem of how that would work in China. The two pictures—the new China and old communist thinking—just don't fit together. In that light, are you a communist, Mr. Zhao? I would say: No. But I should not give the answer if I want to know what you think.

Zhao: Just now you've mentioned Karl Marx's theory. Well, actually in China, before and during the Cultural Revolution, we put much emphasis on the struggle between different classes. Since China launched the policy of reform and opening up, we have already abandoned the so-called class struggle or the struggle between different classes. What we are doing now is trying our best to unite as many people as possible to build China. Since it was founded in the year of 1921, the Communist Party of China (CPC) has set a basic principle, which is "to serve the people." First, the CPC succeeded in the revolution and then it also succeeded in the construction of the country, although in this process it encountered many difficulties and setbacks.

Because I am a member of the CPC, I am certainly a communist. When we are thinking about the prospect of our socialist system, we shall remember Deng Xiaoping's words that China at present is still at the initial stage of socialism, and that it takes several generations, dozens or even scores of generations to strive for the consolidation and development of the socialist system with unremitting efforts. I think it is impossible to give too much detail about the distant future, but the Chinese believe that by the 100th anniversary of the founding of the People's Republic of China, China will have become a mid-level developed country.

John: Yes, of course we very much understand what you said about this, but in the meantime, you know there is a new China, a whole new China, and we are trying to communicate that to the world, the Western world. Every day in the media, on CNN, you'll hear, "Today the communist government of China announces...," "The communist government of China has just decided...," "The communist government of China is using the media. . . . " —every time, universally in the West, old vocabulary. When the West hears "communist government," they still hear in terms of the old vocabulary, the old picture of "communist government," so we do not receive that message "communist government of China" and "this is past. " In the West, they are thinking old pictures, old ideas. So, how can you communicate the new China to the world?

Zhao: I appreciate your in-depth view on this issue concerning how to communicate China's story to the rest of the world. Since you've mentioned CNN just now, I'd like to tell you that I once had a dialogue with Mr. Turner,[①] the founder of CNN. He asked me: "Do you like CNN programs?" I said "No. " Then he asked me why. I said, "You may say your camcorder tells the truth. In Beijing, for example, there are seven sites planted all with beautiful flowers, and also three sites where you see garbage. The CNN reporters videotape the garbage for seven minutes and the beautiful flowers for only three minutes. After seeing the CNN broadcast, the audience in the world will have the conclusion that Beijing is a dirty garbage city. " (John says with a smile, "CNN is often garbage. ") Mr. Turner said: "Well, maybe, but we will make some improvement. " Actually, Asian countries don't seem to like CNN because it is always so picky in reporting the dark side of reality, and even exaggerates it. It is all right to report on the dark side that actually exits, but deliberate exaggeration is not so good.

John: They do the same thing in the United States. And we mentioned in the beginning that for the media only bad news is news.

---

① Ted Turner is the founder of CNN, the largest cable news network in the Unites States. He was vice-chairman of the AOL Time Warner board of directors from 2001 to 2006.

Zhao: Here I think there is an innate prejudice of Western ideology against China under the leadership of the Communist Party of China, and the media are also motivated by commercial interests. Sensational news attracts more audience, which helps media attract more advertising.

Before we have a break, I'd like to ask you a personal question: Because Doris is so knowledgeable, do you feel any threat that some day Doris will surpass you?

John: No, it's a good thing if she passes me. Here is China passing everybody, and here is Doris passing me.

Doris: Never!

Zhao: According to the assessment made by Goldman Sachs,[1] by the year 2027, China's GDP will exceed that of the United States. Suppose Doris represents China and you represent United States, do you feel threatened?

John: No, I'm not threatened by Doris. I'm not threatened by China. I support both.

Dispute between three kinds of consensus

Zhao: A little while ago we talked about the "Beijing Consensus" by

---

[1] Goldman Sachs is a transnational holding company for investment banking and securities. It is one of the Fortune 500 American companies and is headquartered in New York. Its business covers investment banking, securities trading and asset management. It has set up offices in 23 countries and areas of the world.

Joshua Cooper Ramo① in 2004. This is the view held by Mr. Ramo on China and does not represent the official Beijing view. Before that, there was the "Washington Consensus" by Mr. John Williamson,② which was also regarded as the declaration of new liberalism. However, the "Washington Consensus" has not been so successful in guiding economic reforms in Latin American countries. Then Professor Joseph Stiglitz,③ the Nobel laureate in economics, criticized the "Washington Consensus" in his "Post-Washington Consensus." So, in the media people say that there is a debate between three kinds of consensus: the "Beijing Consensus", the "Washington Consensus", and the "Post-Washington Consensus." But actually China has not participated in such a debate.

John: Then why are we talking about it? Could I insert something here? This is all sort of at the academic policy level among certain people. Almost no one in the U. S. was aware of the "Washington Consensus" or the "Beijing Consensus"—almost no one knew about them. They are not very important as a public matter, not very important at all. It was of concern only in small interested circles. In America, we've never seen such a debate. Almost no one cares about it.

---

① Joshua Cooper Ramo is a famous China expert in the United States, formerly a senior consultant to Goldman Sachs, and now managing director at Kissinger Associates, a strategic advisory firm.

② John Williamson is an internationally well-known economist and a senior fellow at the Institute for International Economics. He was a professor of economics at Princeton, MIT and other famous universities in the 1960s and 1970s; his theories of equilibrium exchange rate and exchange target area have been incorporated into textbooks on international economics in the United States and Europe.

③ Joseph E. Stiglitz is professor of economics, commerce, and international and public affairs at Columbia University. He was awarded the Nobel Memorial Prize in Economic Sciences in 2001.

Zhao: Well, thank you for pointing out that the debate has very little influence. In that case, we don't need to spend time and energy discussing it.

John: I think "Washington Consensus" was a consensus of five or six people. (Laughing)

Zhao: Yes, I have noticed that.

John: But what is the idea behind that?

Zhao: The reason the issue of three different kinds of consensus has been raised just now is that I have a concern that some overseas people seem to play up China's road to development. In fact, China has no such intention. However, some people are saying that China is trying to promote its own model to the world. This is not true. There is no such thing. Just now I have said that Chinese philosophy holds that any country should develop in line with its own local conditions and size up the situation before action. No country will succeed if it only copies indiscriminately the practice of others.

John: The way models get passed around is not by someone advocating their own model. The way models get copied is when people are inspired by other people's accomplishments, in this case inspired by China's accomplishments, and want to question whether they couldn't accomplish the same. But the initiative comes from someone who wants to achieve what China has achieved. The initiative always comes from the people who need the model, not the people who have the model. Even if China would try to promote its model to other countries, I would say China is not doing a very good job.

Zhao: Let's again discuss the "China Model." Of course, it is created by China. But we have also learned and benefited from experiences of other countries like the United States, European countries, Japan and Singapore. We have combined their experiences within a Chinese context, and used Chinese culture as the carrier for the creative work. And the result is the so-called "China Model." Now why do we believe we cannot copy the model of other countries? Let me tell you a story to illustrate the point.

The story was told by Yan Zi, an ancient Chinese sage about 2,000 years ago, and collected in *Huai Nanzi*. According to Yan Zi, if you plant tangerine trees south of the Huai River, they will produce tangerines, which taste sour but sweet. If you plant tangerine trees north of the Huai River, tangerines will become trifoliate oranges, which taste sour and bitter. Although both trees seem to have the same leaves, their fruits taste different. Why? Because the soil for their growth is different. ① So the system or the model is just like the tangerine tree and cannot be removed from its own environment.

This is what our ancestors have passed on to us, and often the story that comes from life is closest to the truth.

Doris: It is not easy to understand—from my point of view—why you just cannot have enough self-confidence to look at the Chinese model for what it is. Besides that, your comparison lacks a little bit. You

---

① The story comes from *Yanzi Annals—Inside Volume: A Sequel of the Miscellaneous Collection*. It reads as follows: Tangerines growing to the south of the Huai River become tangerines and those growing to the north of the Huai River become trifoliate oranges. Although they both look similar in foliage, their tastes are quite different. Why? Because of the difference in soil and water.

imported a tangerine; it was a tangerine and didn't become a better tangerine; in other words, you imported Marxism and Marxism didn't become any more practical just because it was practiced in China.

In *China's Megatrends* we describe the principles that are behind the Chinese model. The principles Deng Xiaoping established. He acted like a very wise CEO. There are many parallels between his strategies to guide China into modernity and smart CEOs' measures to get a moribund company back on its feet again. That's how China did it.

The West has a different approach. To take an example, let's look at Afghanistan. Afghanistan and its people were, without question, in bad shape. So to fix Afghanistan, they simply tried to impose Western democracy on Afghanistan. But what the West forgets is that under a superficial Western cover there are still the same Afghan people. The same mindsets. They haven't changed a bit just because a Western cover is thrown over them. The problem is that as long as the basics, the thinking of the people, doesn't change, no real change is possible.

Now what did China do? And that's what you can be really proud of! You did not put a cover over China in the name of ideology. Deng Xiaoping encouraged the people to emancipate their minds so that they could grow on their own. When a plant becomes strong and has taken roots, then it is able to stand on its own, without any backing. So this is what China did and how China at first created the foundation of the system. The problem with the Western model is that it takes away the old foundation of the system it wants to democratize. The West forgets that a new foundation is not built overnight. The smartness in the Chinese system is that no matter how perfect or imperfect it is, it allows itself to grow organically. Deng Xiaoping did not simply throw a new cover over China, or tighten ideological thinking. He did the opposite; he opened the thinking of the people.

Zhao: The gap between ideologies during the Cold War era split the world. It has not been automatically filled up with the end of the Cold War. An example is the stubborn Cold War thinking as shown in Mrs. Thatcher's 2002 book *Statecraft: Strategies for a Changing World*①, in which she insists on criticizing communist China. Deng Xiaoping is a giant to guide the Chinese people to get over the ideological gap. If China had not crossed the gap, it would not have been able to carry out the reform and opening-up policy. This has worldwide significance.

John: He encouraged the people to start making their own decisions again. His call was emancipation, away from indoctrination. America made the huge mistake to think that a country can be changed for the better without taking the minds of the people into account. You, of course, have to win the people to win the battle.

Doris: Very early on, the basic structure, the eight pillars we describe in our book, became the foundation of the new system. As said before, the West, led by the U. S. , takes away the foundation of a system which they want to democratize, whether it is Afghanistan or Iraq. But what is forgotten is that you then need to build a new foundation to replace the old one. That's why there is hardly any bottom-up support by the people in these countries. You cannot turn

① Margret Thatcher, *Statecraft: Strategies for a Changing World* (Harper Perennial, March 2003). In her book, Mrs. Thatcher applies her political experience gained in the 20th century to the analysis of the 21st century, reviews the lesson of the Cold War, describes how the United States has laid the foundation for its superpower status, and explains with the help of her first-hand information the relations between the U. K. and the European Union that have become increasingly strained.

around a country top-down; you need bottom-up support to make reform sustainable. This shows how smart the Chinese strategy is, no matter how perfect or imperfect it is. It helps and engages the people to create the foundation on which the system rests. They are part of the creation; the creation is part of them. Why not tell that to the world? We have an Austrian saying, "Don't put your light under the table."

Zhao: The saying you have quoted is very vivid. There is a similar saying in China, "A bright spot is under a high light." A good book is like a light, illuminating places with temporarily poor visibility.

Doris: My example above shows that it does not work to simply put a cover over something, just as if you put a new coat over an old dress. What China did was to change the system bottom up—not for the sake of a name or for whatever you put over it. The "China Model" does much more than just give an old thing a new name or create a new name for a new thing. It is a process. We talk in our book that we believe China made its steps very carefully, first emancipating the people to stand on their own, to make their own decisions. I think we can get away from the name now and take the next step to look at the Chinese system. What's the structure of the system and how can the world learn from it? What we read most about in the Western media are the things in which China fails, or makes mistakes. But there are many more things that China does very well, and that's the part the West could really learn from.

Seeking common ground while reserving differences

Zhao: You pointed out in your book that the West would like to use its own model as a universal one and ask other countries to follow it. The issue here is whether a given model is universal or not.

Generally speaking, universality has two properties: One is the extension of space, that is, what is applicable in one place is applicable in any other place in the world; the other is the extension of time, that is, what was applicable in the old days is applicable at present, and will be applicable in the future. It is out of question in the field of natural sciences, for example, Newton's three laws and Einstein's theory of relativity. Of course, they are all applicable in China, the United States and Austria, even in Mars and Venus. Therefore, the laws of natural sciences are absolutely universal.

However, we must be very careful in talking about universality in the social sciences. For example, the theory of Professor Keynes[①] played a great role at the beginning of the 1930s during the Great Depression. But in the 1940s the Americans did not follow his theory any longer. Today when we have this global financial crisis, some people are once again turning to the theory of Keynes, but it's no longer appropriate. Thus, we say it is restricted by time and place and there is no universality for it.

Your works over the past years have drawn inferences on social development. In the study of natural sciences, it is comparatively accurate to use the method of extrapolation, under certain conditions, but it's not so for social studies. However, you have comprehensively

---

① John Maynard Keynes (1883-1946) was a British economist, renowned worldwide for spearheading a Keynes' revolution in economic thinking. His representative works include *The General Theory of Employment, Interest and Money* (London: Macmillan Press, & New York: St. Martin's Press, 1936); *Monetary Reform* (London: Macmillan Press, 1924), and *A Treatise on Money* (Harcourt Brace & Co., 1930).

used all your knowledge and wisdom to make an extrapolated anticipation or prediction. That is not easy. This is really a great achievement.

John: I would say that the extrapolation I use is a different kind of extrapolation. Mostly when you say extrapolation, you are thinking about extrapolating data. You have data on the line and you extrapolate it out. What I have been doing is extrapolating ideas.

Zhao: So your method should be called another kind of analytical extrapolation.

John: That could be one name for it.

Doris: I would like to make a step back. You were comparing science and scientific discoveries with rules in our behavior. I think there is a fundamental difference between those and discovering scientific facts. Because whether it was Newton or Einstein, all natural conditions discovered have always been there. They have never changed, and it was only a question of time when we would discover what the truth was or what the facts were and give it a name. And there will be other possible discoveries which we do not yet know. But then there are many things for which there is no absolute truth, and those are the things we create the rules for. We can never create the rules for nature. Whether the Sun moves around the Earth or the Earth moves around the Sun is not within our influence. But we can very much influence the rules under which we live under the Sun, and that's where we can claim to be right or wrong. And that's, of course, the difficulty in building a harmonious global society.

Zhao: But the rules of the world must be acknowledged by most countries of the world. No one can claim that he or she is the representative of truth or the representative of God. During the Warring States Period (475-221 B. C.) more than 2,000 years ago, there were many small kingdoms in China, and the only way for them to solve problems was through wars. They fought wars with each other. Then people were fed up with wars, and some wise men proposed that they should "seek common ground while reserving differences," or "seek common ground on major issues and still reserve differences on minor issues." They did not seek agreement on all issues because it is impossible for people to think in the same way. So in Chinese philosophy, the principles of "seeking common ground while reserving differences" and "harmony being precious" have come down to us since ancient times. Thus, our great thinkers of the past have laid down the tenets for creating a harmonious society.

John: Exactly! Indeed, that's already happening. This formulation you've produced, Mr. Zhao, is very interesting. Because what's happening in the world today is that simultaneously we are globalizing and asserting our cultural identities. And the more we get economically interdependent, the more we get concerned about our cultural identities and the more we celebrate our cultural identities. So it's the same thing; it's integration and diversity, and celebrating our cultural identities as we get closer and closer globally and economically.

Zhao: People around the world tend to believe in their mother culture, skillfully use their mother tongue, and prefer their home cuisine; therefore, some people naturally wish that the world would have the same language and cuisine as theirs. We know that it's absolutely impossible. So I think that the world with cultural pluralism will surely exist for a long time. Recently, the European Union has stressed diversified culture, and I think it has an advanced position on this issue.

John: But the EU is just acknowledging what's already happening in the world anyway.

Doris: I am afraid that we are becoming too loving buddies here. It's as if we were sitting in a pool where we can agree that we can all swim in harmony. The point is that I believe we all are competitive. We are competitive because we always measure everything against something else and we measure our success against somebody else's success; we measure how we look against how somebody else looks; we measure our own culture against another culture. There is always something that is better or worse. And that's the natural condition, which is very hard to overcome in essence.

Zhao: Comparison is not only an important academic approach for scholars, but also a method used by the broad masses of the people to look at problems. However, it is most difficult to reach a consensus on political concepts by comparison, and pluralism in the world political system exists *de facto*. For example, some people regard bipartisanship and parliamentarism as the most reasonable systems and all others wrong. In so doing, they restrict other peoples' freedom of choice and creativity. If they impose their own ideas upon other countries, then conflict will be unavoidable. In the world today, some Western countries demand that China follow or copy their systems. Such a demand is neither reasonable nor acceptable to the Chinese people.

"American Dream," "European Dream," and "Chinese Dream"

Doris: I was raised in Christianity, and there is one sentence in the Bible which comes to my mind, although it is about religion in the context of the Bible. It says: You will recognize them by the fruits they bring forth. [1] Every political system produces certain fruits. But I didn't want to go into that direction just now.

Zhao: Perhaps we can talk about something a bit romantic now: the different dreams of the world. For example, the "American Dream" was once envied and admired by many people in the world, but then there appeared the "European Dream" after the development of the European Union. Many people believe that the "European Dream" would meet their needs more than the "American Dream." So what is the difference between the three dreams: the "American Dream," the "European Dream" and the "Chinese Dream?" The "European Dream" is widely discussed now. A representative work is called *The European Dream*. [2] The author holds that the "European Dream" is a new dream for human development in the 21st century.

John: I know the author. The book is actually about the dream of European socialism.

---

[1] See *The New Testament*, Matthew 7:16, "You will know them by their fruits. Are grapes gathered from thorns, or figs from thistles?" (New York and Glasgow: Collins' Clear-Type Press in *The Holy Bible* published by WM. Collins Sons & Co. Ltd. , p. 6)

[2] Jeremy Rifkin, *The European Dream*, Chinese translator Yang Zhiyi (Chongqing Publishing House, September 2006). In the writer's view, the "European Dream" can set the individual free from the old yoke of Western ideology and at the same time link the human race with a jointly shared new story. It is a dream that leads us in transcending modernity and post-modernity and entering a global age.

Doris: I would like to pick up what you said at the start of the morning session because you said we have a European model; we have European thinking; we have American thinking; and we have Chinese thinking in the model. I was born after World War II, and I grew up in a Europe looking toward the powerful U. S. ; and ever since Europe got out of the rubble of World War II, it has been competing against the "American Dream." Europe wanted to create a "European Dream" that could beat the "American Dream."

Now we have a new situation. We have entered the stage where Europe and America look at China, watching the "Chinese Dream" rising. If we compare the situation with the second half of the 20th century, the U. S. had created an environment that enabled people to make dreams come true. It was economically the most successful country in the world. In Europe, Germany created the so-called the "German Economic Miracle," which you very well know. But it could not question America's role as the land of dreams. Now as the West is declining, China is about to succeed the U. S. as the next land of dreams. I want to see what this dream includes and what China can do to really become this land. No, China doesn't fulfill any other dreams; it allows you to make your own dreams come true. America is a land of unlimited possibilities, and China will become the next land of unlimited possibilities.

Zhao: When we talk about the "Chinese Dream," we could divide it into two stages. The first stage started at the beginning of the 20th century. At that time, China was still under the feudal rule of the emperor of the Qing Dynasty. It was one of the most backward countries in the world. It was even called "a country like a pan of sand," meaning that the Chinese people were not unified during that time. Chinese were called "sick people in East Asia," indicating that the Chinese people were weak both mentally and physically. At that time, people with advanced ideas wanted to overthrow the feudal rule of the emperor. However, after the overthrow of the feudal rule, China entered the stage of wars among warlords and then years of the aggressive war of Japanese militarism. Then "the three big mountains" —the remnants of feudal forces, the imperialist forces in China, and the bureaucratic capitalist forces—lay like a dead weight on the backs of the Chinese people. So the dream for ordinary Chinese people was to overthrow the "three big mountains" and establish a new China. This is the "Chinese Dream" for the first half of the 20th century.

Since the founding of the PRC in 1949, China has enjoyed equality in international political status. However, since it was still left behind in scientific, technological and economic areas, China remained a relatively poor country. During that period, the dream of the Chinese people was to realize modernization of the country and improve their living standard. Today, the "Chinese Dream" can be described more specifically, that is , by the middle of this century China will develop into a "*xiaokang shehui*" ("society of moderate prosperity") in an all-round way, and assume international obligations within its capacity.

John: The leaders always repeat, a "society of moderate prosperity." What is behind the phrase? What is it suggesting? That's an important dream.

Zhao: The concept of "*xiaokang shehui*" was first put forward by Deng Xiaoping, the general designer of the reform and opening up of China, as a call for the comprehensive social progress of China in material, ethical and political civilization. The criteria for material civilization for "*xiaokang shehui*" by the year 2020 can be quantified with some indices, for example , per capita GDP should be over $ 3 ,000 and Engel's coefficient[①] should be under 40% , in addition to other indices for education, health care and environmental protection. It means in the year 2049, when we celebrate the 100th anniversary of the founding of the PRC, the living standard of average Chinese will reach that of a moderately developed country. The "Chinese Dream" is composed of the dreams of all the Chinese people, and will be realized with specific programs and measures in a step-by-step way.

In living standard China still lags far behind the United States and European countries. For example, in terms of car possession per thousand people, the figure is 50 for China, 551 for Austria, which is Doris' country, and 775 for the U. S. , which is John's country, while the global average is 120. Therefore, there is still a long way for China to go.

So, on the one hand, China is still backward as compared with developed countries; on the other hand, there is much more room for China to develop.

John: There's a difference between the U. S. and China that is worth looking at. It is said that in the last half of the 20th century the United

---

① In 1857 Ernst Engel, a German statistician, put forward a view that the less a family's income, the more is the proportion of it spent on food. The view is called "Engel's law" or "Engel's coefficient. " It is expressed as formula: Engel's coefficient (%) = Total expense on food/Total amount of family or individual consumption x 100%. The formula is often used internationally to estimate the living standards of people in a country or region. According to the U. N. Food and Agriculture Organization's standard, the Engel's coefficient > 59% is an indicator for poverty, 50% − 59% for being able to dress warmly and eat one's fill, 40% − 50% for being well-off, 30% − 40% for being rich, < 30% for being very rich.

States became the most successful economy, or in many ways the most successful country in the world. The most interesting thing here for me is that the U. S. is made of all of the people of the world. America is a mix of all of the people of the world, and it became the most successful country in the world. In China we have an alternative picture, and that is that we see an almost completely homogeneous population. What can the difference make in terms of the dreams of the citizens? How do you see that?

Zhao: As you pointed out, the "American Dream" attracted many people in other countries, especially scientists and artists, who were attracted toward the U. S. and also made great contributions to the "American Dream." There were many scientific projects that were done with the help of scientists from other countries. For example, the Manhattan Project[1] benefited from the contributions of Albert Einstein from Germany and Enrico Fermi[2] from Italy, and the American rocket project after World War II also benefited a lot from Wernher von Braun[3] from Germany. Even today, it is said that about one-fourth of the senior experts in science and technology in the United States have come from other countries. Although the majority

---

[1] It is a code name for the study of nuclear weapons by the U. S. army from 1942 on during World War II. The project was headed by American physicist Robert Oppenheimer.

[2] Enrico Fermi (1901-1954), an American-Italian physicist and winner of Nobel Prize in Physics in 1938, was known as the last versatile genius of modern physics. He made great contributions to both theoretical physics and experimental physics. One of the founders of quantum mechanics and quantum theory, he originated the Fermi theory on weak interaction (β decay), was responsible for the design and construction of the first self-sustaining chain fission nuclear reactor of the world, and also was a main leader of the Manhattan Project. The Fermi age theory, Fermi-Dirac distribution, and Fermi level were named after him.

[3] Wernher von Braun (1912-1977) was a German rocket expert, one of the pioneers of the 20th century space enterprise, once a well-known general designer of V-1 and V-2 rockets. He was taken, with his design team, by Americans to the United States after the defeat of Nazi Germany, and he served as the chief designer for the space research and development projects of the National Aeronautics and Space Administration, directing the design of the carrier rocket Saturn 5 for Apollo 4.

of Chinese are of Han people, there are as many as 56 ethnic groups in China. They are natives, unlike in the United States, where so many immigrants came from distant places. I believe there are at least two kinds of difficulty for China to attract foreign talents. First, there is a language problem. Indeed, it is not easy to master the Chinese language. Second, it takes time to improve the living standard and lab conditions in China. However, in the past few years more and more Chinese students who have studied abroad have returned to China. The attraction to them is the dream to rejuvenate China shared by all the Chinese people.

Doris: You are from the scientific world. Economic progress can be proved easily by facts. You can show the world that you have brought 400 million out of poverty, and you have met your economic goals and often overachieved. Everybody can see the cities and buildings of China; the critical point is not the visible modernization or whatever else can be proved by facts and figures. The critical point is that Western thinking includes a certain freedom that is not yet seen in China. But you have made steps in the right direction so that many Western scientists would argue that China is a destination where one cannot make every, but certain dreams come true.

Zhao: A nation's dream is composed of the dreams of all its people. Without the realization of the dreams of a great majority, the national dream will become a castle in the air, a dream that surely will never come into being. The struggle the Chinese people have waged since the beginning of the last century to win national independence in the world is a struggle for democracy and freedom. The realization of democracy and freedom is a process. I have stressed before that the "China Model" or the "China Case" is in the present continuous tense. It is still developing; it is still trying to overcome many difficulties; and it is still far from complete. China really has no intention to promote its own "model" to others.

Doris: I see a certain contradiction here. On the one hand, you want and seek the acknowledgement of the world for what you are; on the other hand, you say you do not necessarily want to be a model. Maybe it is a language problem with the word "model." But if we acknowledge something, a person or a country, we also see certain things we can learn from this person or country, something we can take as a model for things we can improve.

Zhao: Yes, you have pointed out the language issue. I. A. Richards,[1] an early linguist at Cambridge University, found that a serious discussion in the field of the humanities and social sciences would often become a debate on words.[2] A word used by different scholars (not to mention different languages) at different levels of meaning may give rise to ambiguity and vague focus. He proposed that "semasiology" be included into the basic subjects of the humanities and social sciences. New words come out without end in the new era, and it takes time to reach a consensus on their meanings.

The "China Model" vs. the "Western Model"

John: We agree. And even so, the West should look at what it can

---

[1] I. A. Richards (1893-1979) was a British literary critic, poet and representative of new criticism; his works include *The Principles of Literary Criticism* (London: Kegan Paul, Trench, Trubner, 1924); *Science and Poetry* (London: Kegan Paul, Trench, Trubner, 1926); and *Practical Criticism* (London: Kegan Paul, Trench, Trubner, 1929).

[2] Xu Baogeng (Ed.), *Richards: Science and Poetry* (Beijing: Tsinghua University Press, 2003).

learn from the high efficiency your model provides. We cannot afford to stop learning.

In the evolutionary process of creating the "China Model," there are two developments: The leadership, the top, as we call it in our book, is maturing and the bottom is maturing. The top gains more and more confidence about what it has achieved and the appreciation of the Chinese people for those achievements; the bottom gains more self-confidence about how strong it can influence the decisions of the top. I think if we talk about what's lacking, it is a strong transparency in a commonly understood language about what the benefits of the system, of the "China Model," are in comparison with the "Western Model" because the younger generation is not only comparing the "China Model" against China's past, but also against the Western system. But it seems to me from the conversations we have with the young people that the Chinese younger generation wants more transparency, wants to understand why certain decisions are made and also needs a more open dealing with China's past.

Zhao: I appreciate very much the top-down and bottom-up "vertical democracy" mentioned in your book *China's Megatrends*. It is "consultative democracy" if observed from another perspective. How to do it better? We should make more efforts to address the issues relating to it. One of them is the issue of improving transparency. We should improve transparency before policy making and during and after policy implementation so as to improve the policy and the process. Here is an example about traffic regulations. Before China amended its traffic regulations, we held several hearings to collect public opinions, and we also had discussions and collected opinions online. Another example is the amendment to some characters in the Chinese language. Since some scholars proposed to change certain structures of Chinese characters, we put this proposal online, and it met with strong opposition from the overwhelming majority of Chinese netizens. Therefore, the proposal had to be dropped. Problems also arise in the process of implementing a policy. Here is an example of taking over land for development purposes. Since provinces and regions, urban and rural areas, all have very different and complicated conditions, the regulations for taking over land for development need to be further discussed for improvement. This kind of transparency is improving day by day with the help of media, especially the Internet.

In comparison with the West, we do not waste much manpower, time, material or financial resources of taxpayers for that kind of election. The stability of the Chinese government enables its leadership to take a long view of things in a more responsible manner than the frequently changing cabinets in some countries. Chinese leaders would like to say how things will be like in five years or 50 years, whereas the government in some countries might only say how things will go in five months or one year. This is the difference. Therefore, China's development planning is based on strategic considerations, and the government must have a long-term sense of responsibility.

Of course, there are also shortcomings in our work, and we need improvement in such issues as how to exercise better supervision over the ruling party and government and how to overcome the frequently occurring cases of corruption. These issues have posed a real challenge to the ruling party. But we will not dodge this challenge and will make more efforts in the following areas: 1) severely punish unlawful behavior; 2) improve and reinforce the existing supervisory mechanism; 3) have more transparency. In observing things, we need to have both a historically vertical approach and a worldwide horizontal approach. It is beyond question that comparison is an important means to recognize problems.

Doris: Let's come back to democracy. What you have said could help Chinese as well as Westerners to gain a better understanding of China. What we suggest is that China does not only need marketing for the country to the outside world, but marketing to the inside, to the Chinese themselves.

Yesterday, I talked to a young man, a quite smart guy. I asked, "How would you describe your political system?" And he said, "Not so free." I quickly drew a graph to show the comparison between the Chinese model and Western democracy. The graph was a drawing of party A and party B. Then he said "Oh, freedom of choice!" I said "Yes, freedom of choice, but for the freedom of choice, you pay a price. Party A blames party B for being all wrong and party B tries to prove party A wrong." Then the young man said, "Oh yes! You are right." It was something he wasn't really aware of.

I think many people are not aware of the advantages the Chinese model offers for the Chinese. You can go forward; you don't need to quarrel and you don't need to lose time. If John and I had been acting like party A and party B, we would have been quarrelling all the time and we would have never got the book done. The output is so much better if you act in favor of the matter than in favor of a certain opinion.

John: We should mention the last sentence this guy nevertheless added. He said, "If you always have to be right, how can you learn?" And here is where China needs a lot more transparency. We do not believe that in the Chinese leadership everybody has the same view on everything. But different opinions at a certain point are put aside to find a common strategy. We believe the leadership, at least the top, doesn't have to be always right, but has to do the best to serve the country. They make mistakes; they might go wrong on some things and they might have to step back and start again. But they are doing their best. If that is understood, this is a much better foundation than any election.

Zhao: I think you present your views in a very convincing manner. I think your views are not only beneficial to the Chinese young people but also inspiring for me. Given China's unique historical background and current national conditions, I think it is an appropriate choice to practice socialism with Chinese characteristics. The Western system and various other systems are all selected by corresponding countries on their own.

If we review history, we can see that in a given historical period, bipartisanship or multiparty elections actually failed to achieve the results as the ideal of democracy aspired. Instead, they only became a placebo for voters' democratic claims. In the 1930s, for example, German people elected Mr. Hindenburg,① who had been a general during World War I, to be president. It was reported that at presidential meetings, he would surprise everybody present by suddenly uttering remarks about the war situation of World War I and about where to deploy his army. But Hitler was pleased to see that, because he knew this president could be under his complete control. Of course the probability of such a case in history is rare, but even if

---

① Paul von Hindenburg (1847-1934) was a field marshal and politician of Germany and the second president of the Weimar Republic. During his tenure of office, the country was politically unstable and economically depressed. In 1933 he appointed Adolf Hitler prime minister and helped him come into power.

it happens once in decades or 100 years, human beings will pay a very high price for it. By saying this, I do not mean that I'm opposed to bipartisanship in other countries. I do not have the right to vote in other countries, and I only want to say it does not suit the conditions of China.

As for the errors committed by the CPC in its history, we have to see that the Party has not only bravely admitted those errors, but also seriously analyzed the subjective factors and social causes for their occurrences. To learn lessons from history, the Party has also issued party resolutions and made them public. One example is Resolution on Certain Questions in the History of the Chinese Communist Party since the Founding of the People's Republic of China. ①

John: Looking at single cases, we can prove almost everything right or wrong. While India is called the biggest democracy in the world— which we would question for several reasons, but that's another matter—economically people are much better off in China. How much

---

① The Sixth Plenary Session of the Eleventh Central Committee of the Chinese Communist Party held in June, 1981, examined and approved the Resolution on Certain Questions in the History of the Chinese Communist Party Since the Founding of the People's Republic of China. In the resolution the CPC Central Committee applying Marxist dialectical materialism and historical materialism made a correct summation of the major events, particularly the Cultural Revolution, in the history of 32 years since the founding of the People's Republic of China, scientifically analyzed the correct and erroneous ideas in the guiding ideology of the Party, analyzed the subjective factors and socio-historical causes for error occurrences, correctly and fairly judged some Party leaders' merits and demerits, realistically evaluated and affirmed the importance of Mao Zedong's historical role in Chinese revolution and construction, and fully expounded the great significance of Mao Zedong Thought as the guiding ideology of the Chinese Communist Party.

This resolution and the Resolution on Certain Questions in the History of the Chinese Communist Party in 1945 are regarded as the two most important and authoritative historical documents within the Party since its founding in 1921, and both have performed great functions in making conclusions to some controversial questions in the history of the Party, comprehensively summarizing the historical experience of the Party, reaching a common understanding among all members of the Party, and providing guiding theory for the Party development in the future.

does voting mean to you if you cannot feed your children? Things can go wrong either way in a vertical or in a horizontal democracy.

Doris: The only point we see as a bigger risk in the Chinese system is that if the Chinese leadership is bad, it's very bad for China. If party A in the horizontal democracy governs badly, it is dropped in the next election.

But as someone explained to us, Chinese see things in a bigger dimension, in a historical context. If the system is bad, it will be gone in the long run. As we all agree, the "China Model" is a model in progress. It shows results that are unquestionable. But as in business, the memory for good things is short. What counts is the present.

Zhao: The Cultural Revolution is an example of serious errors made by the CPC and also a great lesson for the Party. How to avoid making such errors again is an important task for party building. In fact, to describe our system more precisely, China practices a multi-party cooperation system under the leadership of the CPC. Besides the CPC, we have other parties in China. They not only participate in government administration and state affairs, but also exercise democratic supervision over the CPC. This is their one important function. What is more important to me is the belief that any social system is doomed to failure if it is not supported by the people. This has been proved by human history and will continue to be proved in the future.

Doris: From the long-term perspective, it is right; however, from the short-term perspective, sometimes it is not the case.

Zhao: In other words, what kind of citizens will determine what kind of government they have. If the citizens have a strong sense of being the masters of the country, they will not tolerate a government which goes against the will of the people. This should be the truth.

John: We've written about that in our book. We think the present model is well in place and it is just a beginning. It has a long way to run and all the indications so far are in a medium term. I see it in favor to continue, because of the great widespread support from the citizens, because of the outstanding unprecedented success of the model. There's no reason to assume that in the short or medium term the model will not develop further, become more mature as the people themselves become more mature and sophisticated. It will take a long time before getting close to perfection, but the direction is firmly set to see a successful future.

Part Two

On the Global Understanding of China

China at the center of the world stage

Zhao: Just now we have mentioned the Western media. We do not want to assume Western journalists' reports to be biased. But nevertheless we cannot ignore the fact that quite a number of articles hold on to an obsolete picture of China or selectively focus on negative occurrences. Few people have experienced China first-hand. Thus most people have to rely on what they hear or read about it. What do both of you think are the causes for the obsolete picture and misunderstandings of China? What are the issues that should be addressed by China?

John: I have to bring you to the stark truth of the matter: Most ordinary people in other countries do not have a real interest in China. If you live in Austria, Switzerland, or in Texas or California of the U. S. , you have your own problems and your own concerns that are really immediate, like your family, the mortgage on your household, sports news and other matters. People are most interested in things that have direct impact on their lives. Human beings are interested in 20 or 40 things for the most part. In the meantime we have to say that in recent years, as China undergoes political and economical changes and developments, the country becomes much more important in the international arena; so more and more people, not everyone, are going to become more interested. This might be a starting point from which to take actions.

Zhao: Many years ago China was on the margin of the global stage. For example, in discussing post-war issues during the later period of World War II, the leaders of the United States, the United Kingdom and the former Soviet Union met at the Yalta Conference, but the leaders of China were excluded from such an important meeting that determined the issues relating to the core interests of China after the war. However, since the founding of the PRC, especially over the past three decades, China has gradually moved from the margin to the center of the world stage and played a more and more important role in international affairs. Although the number of ordinary people interested in China may be relatively small in the West, many people in the political and media circles have paid great attention to China because what has happened in China will make a significant impact on the world. Look at China itself. Twenty or 30 years ago, little international news and few commentaries on international affairs could be found in general newspapers, except big ones such as *People's Daily* or *China Daily* in China. So during that period of time many Chinese people did not pay much attention to international affairs. However, as China enhances its importance on the world stage and the effect of world changing situation on China is heightened, Chinese people begin to take interest in foreign affairs. When people had no U. S. dollars, they didn't care about the exchange rate between RMB and USD. Now many people have U. S. dollars and they become interested in the dollar trend, though they look at it from different perspectives. The overseas population that takes interest in China also begins to expand slowly from the top to the bottom of society. I think things go like this.

Doris: I disagree with what John has said that only few people are interested in China. It seems to me that they are interested in different ways. I'd like to use a metaphor. Picture the world as a big neighborhood. China for a long period was in a way out of sight, living in the suburbs, so people did not pay too much attention to China. But to their surprise, China now moves right into the middle of their neighborhood. And not only that, China, this new neighbor, starts to raise his voice. So what do all the old neighbors do? They do what everybody else does when new neighbors move in. They gossip! And for gossip you do not need facts. The less you know, the more imaginative the rumors are. "Did you hear? I think the man was beating his wife. " "Look at their children. They hardly say anything because their parents are oppressing them. " So the gossip is floating. But what is the truth about the new neighbor? Good advice to that new neighbor would be to open their doors, invite the old neighbors in and say, "This is our family and this is how we are. This is how we live. These are the rules we have in our family. " Then the families who visit the new neighbor will realize that some or many things differ from the gossip. An open dialogue between the old and the new neighbor will help to clarify misinterpretations and support understanding where opinions differ.

Telling neighbors the true story

John: In my book *High Tech High Touch*[1] I wrote that when you introduce a new species into any ecological environment, it will change the relationships within the environment. As Doris said, when China emerged in the global neighborhood, the old neighbors, the established political powers, started to gossip too. The more influential the "new neighbor," the more extensive the gossip.

---

[1] John Naisbitt, *High Tech High Touch*, Chinese translator Yin Ping (Science Press, 1979). The author anticipates that in the scientifically developed society, enterprises that take human characteristics into account will become the megatrend of development for Asia and even the whole world in the future. Genetic engineering is more revolutionary than the computer industry in that it can decide the future and enable the human race to control the process of its own evolution.

Zhao: What a vivid analogy to illustrate the point! When China comes to the center of the world stage, he should tell his neighbors what to be done at home or to the surrounding environment. All this needs to be regularly released to the outside world. About seven or eight years ago, the ministries and local governments of China didn't have any regular press conferences. They have carried out a reform with the effect of holding regular press conferences to provide domestic and international media with information on new policies and newly happened things in China without delay.

In the past we have been reluctant to tell our story or have not been good at telling our story; that made it easier, therefore, for people in other countries to create their own versions of China's story. Their stories may deviate from the truth. And we know that once a prejudice is built, it is hard to correct, and this is true both at home and abroad. Now China begins telling its story regularly, and it is telling the true story. If a story is not true, it is better not to tell it because it could cause even more damage.

Sometimes even with the true story, Chinese may speak *Chinglish* in the Chinese way of thinking, which cannot be understood by overseas people. For example, in China there is a moving love story against feudal oppression called *Liang Shanbo and Zhu Yingtai* (Chinese Romeo and Juliet), which has been adapted for an opera in *Wu* dialect in Jiangsu and Zhejiang provinces of China. If the opera is performed in its local dialect in Beijing, Beijingers cannot understand it, let alone overseas people if it is performed abroad. When the opera was adapted for a violin concerto, it was very successful, circulating abroad as *Butterfly Lovers*.

Finding a topic of common interest

Doris: I would like to answer with a metaphor again. The Eskimos live in a snow environment; therefore, they have about 30 different words for snow. The Tuaregs are living in the desert of the Sahara, so they have about 30 different words for sand and stone. When an Eskimo and an African desert person talk about the danger and conditions of the environment, one is thinking of the danger of ice and snow, and the other is thinking about the danger of no water in endless dunes. To communicate they need a common language. They have to thrash out the difference and meet the challenge for a picture they both can understand, like surviving in an misanthropic environment. Both are struggling in their own way.

Zhao: If we discuss this problem with our university students, they will be very interested in it and go deep into the connotation of "context." In fact, some words used by Chinese are totally identical with their counterparts used by Westerners in definition, for example , material nouns like "atom," "molecule," "desk" and "chair." Once expressions are related to thinking, or human emotions, there is a great difference between Chinese and Western words in interpretation. For example, Hegel's *Philosophy of History*① was originally written in German. When it was translated into English, in the foreword the translator placed great emphasis on the difference between German and English in words like "intelligence," "will" and "mind" ("Geist" in German), words that have no one-to-one correspondence in

---

① Georg Wilhelm Friedrich Hegel, *Die Philosophie der Weitgeschichte*, English translator J. Sibree (Dover Publications, 1956); Chinese translator Wang Zaoshi (Shanghai Bookstore Publishing House, 2006).

translation. Therefore, he said he had tried his best but there was still some difference between the English and the German version of Hegel's book. *The Philosophy of History* is *Die Philosophie der Weltgeschichte* donned in English apparel. Actually, German is closer to English than French and some other languages. Even with such affinitive languages as German and English, the translator still had insurmountable difficulties. Thus, we may conceive that due to the great difference between Chinese and Western languages as well as the existence of untranslatability in language and culture, it would be much more difficult for both Chinese and Westerners to communicate successfully in dialogue.

Doris: I can't agree with you more. Peter Sloterdijk,[1] a German philosopher, once wrote that people do not want to learn something new, but only want to listen to things that confirm their preconceived opinions.

Zhao: Good quote. Reviewing old lessons without learning new is a deviation from the cognitive process that should be avoided. In fact, many definitions of words in dictionaries used by Chinese are different from those in dictionaries used by Americans and Europeans. Take "market economy" as an example. About 30 years ago, the Chinese held that "market economy" belonged to capitalism and was a backward social system. But it is different now. There is a change in its interpretation in Chinese dictionaries today; therefore, it facilitates people to better understand capitalism. One more example is Max

---

① Peter Sloterdijk (1947-) is a professor of philosophy and president of the State Academy of Design at the University of Karlsruhe and his works include *Critique of Cynical Reason* (Minneapolis: Minnesota Press, 1988), and *Rage and Time* (New York: Columbia University, 2010).

Weber's book *The Protestant Ethic and the Spirit of Capitalism.* ①

John: It's a very good book.

Zhao: In the past, we have rarely read any book like this. Now China starts to adopt a lot of measures for market economy under the guidance of Deng Xiaoping. In reality we have changed the definition of "market economy" formulated 30 years ago.

John: I have another example. About a year ago, in 2008, I was in Tianjin University talking to a group of students. At that time, obviously the international financial crisis was growing. A student asked me how the U. S. would deal with this crisis in comparison with how they dealt it in the 1930s. I thought for a little while and said, "Well, now they become socialist. "

For example, they might pour money into obsolete and nonviable enterprises, just to keep the jobs. This is a socialist measure. In a sentence, now China has a market economy with Chinese characteristics, and the U. S. is moving toward a socialist economy with American characteristics! So China is moving and America is moving too. They might meet at some point.

---

① Max Weber (1864-1920) was a German political economist and sociologist acknowledged as one of the important founders of modern sociology and public administration. *Die Protestantische Ethik und der Geist des Kapitalismus* (Beltz-Athenaeum, July 2000) holds that religion is one of the main reasons for the disparity between the East and the West in cultural development, and it stresses the important role of the Protestant Ethic in the development of capitalism, bureaucracy and legal authority.

Not judging another culture by your own measures

Zhao: Only when the communication between China and the Western world becomes a cross-cultural one as mentioned just now can it produce a good effect. The Chinese people need to have the cross-cultural communication capacity and so do the Western people. Neither side should look at the other's culture with quite different eyes. This makes it easy for one to understand the real life situation of the other, including its real mentality and true ideas.

In order to overcome the difficulties in cross-cultural communication, one has to overcome the inertia of thinking. Take a look at China. Because the CPC is the ruling party in China, many Western politicians cannot get rid of the Cold War mentality and its disappearance is really very slow. The worst is that they even look at China with the view they used in observing the former Soviet Union in the time of Stalin and Truman, and this is unavoidably erroneous.

The ideological gap may lead to prejudice. Once I had a dialogue with the leader of an American Jewish organization. I said, "I have great respect for two outstanding Jews in history: One is Karl Marx, and the other is Albert Einstein." His reply was, "No. You are only 50 percent right." While many people in other nations hold that Marx was at least a great thinker, the respondent, as a Jew, did not recognize and even negated Karl Marx as an excellent representative of the Jewish people completely out of ideological differences.

John: Yes. It's funny. I've never heard that before.

Doris: We are talking about a rather complex issue now. To simplify, I will go back to my example of the "new neighbor." The new neighbor might carry some burdening baggage from the past. Maybe someone in the family has made serious mistakes. You have several ways to handle it: You cover up the past; you only talk about the good things; or you admit there were good things and bad things. For the old neighbors who point at the new neighbor and say, "You have these dark spots on your history," they might forget that they have dark spots as well and it took them 50 years to speak openly about them. But nevertheless they want the new neighbor to present his mistakes on a silver tray right away.

Zhao: This reminds me of Confucius' words, "Virtue does not go with isolation; it will win good neighbors."[①] The Chinese people believe that virtuous conduct will win neighbors' understanding and help establish good relationships.

After the Austrians have a correct understanding of that particular period in their history, it will bring Austria new honor. As a Chinese saying goes, "Put down the burden and continue moving forward." Sometimes both Germans and Austrians may humorously say that Hitler was not their countryman but Beethoven was.

As you prefer the example of neighbors, I'd like to go further on it. Suppose some family in a community has an internal problem and they're probably going to divorce because of it. At this moment the best way to get the family together is to quarrel with their neighbors. When there is a conflict with their neighbors, the internal trouble will disappear. For example, after the financial crisis, two important

---

① From *The Analects of Confucius*: *Inside Benevolence*.

financial figures in the U. S. blamed it on China for the reason that China had bought so large a quantity of U. S. bonds that Americans felt they were rich and went on shopping sprees. So let's come back to the example of neighbors. When a family has some internal trouble, it is a good method to solve the problem by having a bone to pick with the neighbors (John laughing).

Doris: You are absolutely right. When the Soviet Union broke apart, the biggest problem for the U. S. was that it had lost its enemy.

John: I once had a private talk with a Russian official. He said that in Moscow Gorbachev once said to an American, "We are going to do a terrible thing to you; we are going to take away your enemy." Because when the Soviet Union fell apart, America lost its enemy and its scapegoat.

Making money from a negative story of China

Zhao: Some Western media fail to have a correct understanding of China and concentrate on any negative story about China they come across. They are doing so for commercial considerations because newspapers with negative sensational stories sell best. In addition, they cultivate a readership that loves to read negative stories about China, and conversely this readership also helps the media to continue carrying negative reports on China. The media cultivate their readership, and the readership cultivates the media as well. This holds true for such Japanese camera companies as Canon and Nikon. They keep saying that for digital cameras, a model with a hundred thousand pixels is not so good and it is better to have a model with a million pixels for quality pictures. Therefore, customers give up the former and buy the latter. Then the companies tell the customers that a model with ten million pixels is even better. So the customers will ask the camera companies to produce the new model with more pixels. What the camera companies say may not be wrong and in this way they keep on making money. It seems to me that some Western media like to publish some sensational news just out of commercial interests in order to attract more readers. But they are different from the camera factories in that their news or commentaries are not objective or fair.

John: I don't think China bashing per se increases profits that much. It is a pretty good theory and some people might agree. But I think it's beside the point. The point is sensationalism, and sensationalism can be associated with celebrities, and it also can be associated with countries, you know, the whole crazy stuff. For example, the lead in the children's toys made in China. It was just a tiny part for China, which is the largest toy supplier in the world. They made such a big deal about it because it was a sensational story. And I think it's a function of sensationalism whether it has to do with surprise in Hollywood or some commercial activities or something outrageous. They think it's outrageous to China that the category here is sensationalism. I don't think we are going to better understand China because that will increase our profits. What we increase our profits with is being sensational in every regard including China.

Zhao: Well, I'm very glad to hear that you disagree with me on my view, because without a conflict we could not have a wonderful dialogue. But in the later part your explanation seems close to mine (laughing with John).

Winning respect with one's own capability or effort

Zhao: Well, just now the organizer of this dialogue gave me a note reminding me that John and I are both advanced in years and we should have a break. I am very happy that we're allowed a break, but don't tell me that we're old. I think you and I are as energetic as they (pointing at Doris and Mr. Zhang Hongbin, the interpreter). What do you think?

Doris: Age is not the problem. Both of you seem quite animated. I didn't notice that anybody paid attention to age.

Zhao: Well, in China the elderly usually earn more respect from people. I'm wondering whether it is the same in Austria.

Doris: The respect for the elderly is not very high in Austria, and you do not get credit just because you are old. To be honest, being older does not necessarily mean being wiser. There are dim-witted young people, and there are unwise old people. One might be a little more polite or gentler when dealing with a person of age. But you do not earn any credit just because you are some years older than others.

Zhao: I don't think John totally agrees with what you have just said. He might believe that wisdom usually grows with age.

John: Actually I totally agree with Doris. For the most important thing Doris said is that we have to earn respect in how we live our lives and what we do. It can't be given chronologically.

Zhao: It's true that old age is not something to be relied upon. Of course, the elderly, on the other hand, are respected for their contributions to society. Our views approximate the convergence here.

Part Three

How to Tell China's Story Better

Telling China's story in a brand-new language

John: Well, let's pick up where we stopped yesterday and move on. We've talked about telling China's story several times and wondered if China is doing a good job in telling its story. I'm not sure that we have to urge China to tell a story better. I think the answer is that you have to train people who tell China's story in a better way. If more people can come to China and write about China, the world may get different versions. I think China should be more transparent, invite more people in, encourage more people to talk and examine what's going on and tell the world about it. In short, China needs to sell itself and its achievements better to the world.

Zhao: I totally accept your suggestion. Overseas people who would like to tell China's story need Chinese—just like your friend and author Ms. Haihua Zhang—to tell them something about China. But right now there are not many Chinese who can communicate fluently in other languages. I am dean of the School of Journalism at Renmin University of China, which is one of the best universities in China. I'm training students, helping them to improve their ability to tell China's story, including the ability to communicate with foreigners. I'd like to invite you and Doris to our school to give a lecture to hundreds and thousands of students there. It surely will be sensational.

John: From your lips to the students' ears. We'd be happy to go there. We know your university is very good and we know you do a good job in that university. We'd love to do the lecture. I think the problem you have is that Chinese are stuck in an old vocabulary. It's a paradox to tell today's story in yesterday's words. You need to bust out the old vocabulary to tell the story well.

Hearing the truth for the first time

Zhao: Yesterday I gave you a book[①] which describes how sometimes both Chinese and people in other countries find it difficult to bridge the cultural gap or iron out cultural disparity in their communications. It is not only a language problem but also a cultural problem. It takes great efforts to solve the problem.

Doris: You are right. But sometimes we are surprised in a positive way. Yesterday we read an interview on our book *China's Megatrends* published in a German magazine with not too much of a negative undertone. What was really surprising were the readers' comments on the article. More than 80 percent of them were positive. One comment was, "Finally somebody has said the truth!" That's just a quick report on the first media reaction. That might change and we expect negative comments as well. We should also mention the experience we had in Finland, where we met with government people, media, academics from America and Finland and many representatives from the corporate world. There was such a hunger for the real picture of China, for facts instead of opinions. It has encouraged us to gain a better understanding of China, and we hope we can count on your support, even if we touch controversial matters.

Zhao: I encourage you to ask any question you have. And

---

① It refers to the book *In One World—101 Stories in Communication with Overseas People* by Zhao Qizheng, (Liaoning Education Press, 2007).

congratulations to you! Perhaps yours is the first German book written by a non-Chinese for a truthful description of today's China with in-depth explanations and comments.

Complementing differing philosophies

Zhao: I hope you don't mind, Mr. Naisbitt, but Chinese have a special respect for Germans—perhaps due to the fact that there are so many philosophers born in Germany and Chinese also like philosophy. So in the eyes of the Chinese, well-educated German people are like philosophers. I don't think you're unhappy about what I have said.

John: No, no. I agree with you. Germany has the great tradition of philosophical thinking, and many excellent philosophers come from Germany.

Zhao: "The Germans" here refers to all German-speaking people, including German-speaking Austrians. Language itself is culture, and also a most important carrier of culture.

Doris: Oh! Thank you very much.

John: Also let me add something here. I'm American and I know America has produced very few philosophers. Why is that? The question remains open for further research. The fact is that there are very few world-class philosophers from America.

Zhao: Americans often say that they have a short history of 200 years only. In my view, it cannot be put this way. Actually the United

States has inherited European culture, particularly Martin Luther's[1] Protestant spirit, although not all European traditions. Therefore, its capitalism has developed very fast, as pointed out by Max Weber. Usually a culture that overemphasizes pragmatism will lead to the neglect of philosophy. This is true not only for the United States, but also for other countries.

John: We have to keep in mind that China has a great tradition of philosophers. Many of the great philosophers, including some outstanding contemporary ones, come from China. My question here is whether the tradition is being carried on.

Zhao: While there are differences between Chinese philosophy and Western philosophy which originates from ancient Greek philosophy, they are complementary. Western philosophy pays more attention to conceptual thinking in logical deduction; therefore, it is of great significance for thinking in natural sciences, whereas Chinese philosophy pays more attention to ethics; therefore, it emphasizes harmonious relations between the human race and nature. The two philosophies should complement each other.

It's not true to say that there is no American philosophy in the United States. But they need philosophers to extract and refine it. For example, Americans are far ahead of others of the world in innovative spirit. They could take the lead in landing on the Moon, not once, but twice. They also could explore Mars. Up to now all this can only be achieved by the United States, and such acts come from the philosophical ideas as their basis. It's a pity that nobody has refined it

---

[1] Martin Luther (1483-1546) was an advocate of religious reform in Europe in the 16th century and founder of the Lutheran denomination of the Protestant faith.

so far. Mr. Naisbitt, if you take on American philosophy in the future, you'll make a great success. It'll be your second success.

John: (Laughing) Is that my assignment?

Zhao: No. I think that since you have pointed out the unexplored field, it would be a pity if you passed onto others what you're capable to do in this field. You're in a very good position to do so, because you not only know America, know Europe, but also know China. Only through such a comparison of world affairs can one become a good philosopher. Without comparison, there'll be no good philosopher.

Jointly promoting the product of China

John: Thank you for your suggestion. I was going to say something about different philosophers in China. Deng Xiaoping, of course, was not a philosopher, or poet, or idealist. He was a great reformer and popularizer, a popularizer of philosophy. In formulating China's strategy of reforms, he used the great philosophical saying, "We have to cross the river by feeling for the stones." That is a wonderful summary of the task ahead for China. China crossed a river it had never crossed before, moving to a better future. He understood what would resonate among Chinese people.

Doris: Now I think we have clarified our roles. John is the philosopher and I'm the salesperson. Since we're sitting here to sell a product called China, John will make its framework of ethical values and I'll try to point out its practical value. In this way we can make a very good team and continue to be a very good team.

Zhao: We have much admiration, not jealousy of such a good family like yours. Now I'd like to pick up what you've said earlier about creating new words to describe new things. Due to the uniqueness of Chinese characters, the creation of new words in Chinese is not as easy as in Romanized languages. Americans are good at coining new words. For example, the American policy on China is described by a well-known think tank[1] as "congagement," that is, a new word formed with the clipped elements of "containment" and "engagement." I've asked an American political personage about this word and he said that the meaning of the new word is "contact with containment."[2] It seems to me that the meaning of the new word is comparable to the power brake of a car with an automatic transmission: Containment when the brake is on and engagement when the brake is off, as is determined by American interests. How to put "congagement" into a concise Chinese word? It takes some thinking.

In the process of our dialogue, the topic may vary with the change of our interest. Just as I pointed it out in my email to you, we seem to be visiting a big garden, and we can go anywhere we wish with a variance in our mood and scene.

Have you ever been to the Summer Palace? There are artificial hills, screens, woods and a long corridor. Where shall we go? Just follow our inclinations.

---

① A think tank is an organization engaged in the investigation, analysis and study of political, commercial and military policies, usually independent of government and political parties; many think tanks have relationships with laboratories, universities and military and business institutions, and some carry the name of "research institute."

② A strategy between blockade and contact; after its proposal, it was systemized to some extent by the study and validation of some U. S. institutes of strategic research and accepted by the Bush Administration; it generally means that while promoting the integration of the Chinese economy into the global economic system, the U. S. will not give up political or even military means to contain China so as to prevent China from constituting a threat in any form to the U. S.

John: Great! So let's talk about Tibet.

Zhao: Good idea!

Telling the truth of Tibet to the world

John: In terms of economic development, everybody can see the buildings that have been built, the visible modernization of China; but when it comes to other fields, it is a different picture. What you read in the Western press is not how many schools have been built in Tibet. What you read in the Western media is that Tibetan people have been turned down. I believe that just as much as economic progress in other parts of China becomes transparent, it should be known that China is not putting those people down or oppressing the Tibetan people, and human rights are also available to Tibetan people. We will very much appreciate it if you can give us more evidence to rebut those arguments, because we have only a little knowledge about Tibetan history, but what we have learned is quite a different story than the one told by the West. We need information from you to argue against one-sided impressions of the situation of the Tibetan people, and comment on Western media reports on riots in Tibet or Urumqi.

Zhao: Indeed, there are many distorted views among Western people on the issues of Tibet and Xinjiang. In addition to the serious distortion of truth in Western media's reporting, China also should take some responsibility. Sometimes in the past it did not report these issues in time and their transparency was not enough. When I was Minister of the State Council Information Office, we did a very important job, that is, to encourage all the ministries, provincial governments and the governments of municipalities directly under the Central Government to set up a press release system. If we do not tell the truth, Western media may just guess, and they will interview those people who are not satisfied with China. The delay on our side may go so far as to provide enough time for distorted reports or rumors to circulate. Once they made an impression on people, it becomes difficult to change it because the first impression remains strongest.

Had foreign journalists been there to cover the incident when the violence occurred in Lhasa on March 14, 2008, the world would have known more about the true story then and there. It was a pity that they had no opportunity to conduct interviews on the spot then. But this time an improvement has been made in dealing with the "7/5 Incident" in Urumqi by allowing foreign journalists to conduct free interviews there. So their coverage of the incident in Urumqi is closer to the truth than the last one in Tibet.

Take Tibet as an example. There is a very famous weekly called *Stern* in Germany. Recently it has published a long article saying that the Western understanding of Tibet is mainly based on the following points: a) Tibet is a place like Shangri-La; b) Tibet was occupied by the Chinese army at the beginning of the 1950s; c) The Dalai Lama is the leader of the Tibetans and he is a religious figure. Concerning the first point, it is right to say that Tibet is like Shangri-La because it is really beautiful. But the second point is totally wrong because Tibet has been part of China's territory ever since the 13th century when China was in the Yuan Dynasty 800 years ago. As for the third point, the Dalai Lama is by no means as simple as a religious leader. He's a separatist in nature. Some of his speeches seem to be about Buddhism, and some actually attack our Tibetan policies. He supports the forces for "Taiwan independence" and "Xinjiang independence," and the core of all his activities is intended to split China. The so-called "Greater Tibet" he attempts to establish is equivalent to one-fourth of the total territory of China.

I believe the best way to better understand and have an in-depth study of Tibet is to make an onsite investigation there and talk to many people face to face.

Doris: You just explained your views, and we also have plans to visit Tibet. We have also read the article in *Stern*. And it was for a long time, ever since I can remember, the first article that was scratching on the myth that people in Tibet had lived in paradise before the Chinese came back to Tibet. So that was a very positive article; and in regard to the history of Tibetan peasants, it was also a somewhat terrifying article on this matter. Nevertheless, of course, the article adds at the end "yes-but," which is the case in almost every article about China.

In this regard, what we write in the book is not only talking in our own words, we are also quoting from a Stanford professor from Taiwan who asked, "How can China win the PR battle against that ever-smiling man who has never had to prove anything?" And I say that it's like a political opposition party, which always says, "The government doesn't do this and that; if we were in power, we would do all of this and the people would be much better-off." But the opposition will not have to fulfill all the promises, as we have experienced many times in Western democracy. Once an opposition gets into power, it is most likely that nothing happens and the promises fade away.

So the point is that the Dalai Lama is in a decade long "opposition" to China. That makes it a lot easier for him. It is obvious that all the Dalai Lama needs to do is to appear and talk about Tibet, and China reacts like a bull in the Spanish bullfight facing a red flag. He raises the red flag and the bull comes running. China comes running and fuming, and the West has all the reason to say, "Well, see, we are right here; they are coming again." And that's kind of the trap into which China steps every time the Dalai Lama pulls out his flag. I wonder what would happen if he were ignored. It always needs two parties to act and react. And China is always reacting to the Dalai Lama. Why can't China take action and launch a sort of image campaign about the truth of Tibet and the truth of the Dalai Lama.

And I also think, but this is my very private opinion, if you nail the Dalai Lama down in dialogue, he cannot kick back. Fareed Zakaria[1] interviewed the Dalai Lama for CNN and quoted his own words that Tibet should go back to the Tibetans. Zakaria added that the "Greater Tibet" claimed by the Dalai Lama for his people is quite some part of China, and he asked the Dalai Lama how much of China he claimed. The Dalai Lama was giggling. He didn't give a complete answer, but "ha, ha, ha," or "yes, but not all." He escaped answering the question and Fareed Zakaria did not push it. When we met Fareed Zakaria later at a conference in Russia and we asked him why he had not insisted on an answer from the Dalai Lama. He said: "He is an old man." As much as it is an honor if someone respects the "weakness" of an "old man," we wonder if Zakaria would have been as gentle with a 74-year-old Chinese politician.

---

① Fareed Zakaria is an American-Indian scholar. He is a host for CNN, an editor for *Newsweek International*, and the author of *The Post-American World*.

Zhao: One important reason for the "success" of the Dalai Lama in public relations is that he has got the support of some given forces. He lobbies everywhere and the only objective of his PR activities is to advocate "Tibet independence." The topics of his speeches are frequently something like "be merciful at heart" or "what happiness is." He does not put politics in the headline, but in the content. So when people begin to like the Dalai Lama and his words, they will like his claims and fall into the traps he has set. His method is very tactful.

To my surprise, we read the same article in the weekly *Stern* in different places.

Actually, we exercise bilingual education in Tibet. In order to protect the development of the Tibetan language, we have particularly set up Tibetan schools on top of Mandarin schools. In Tibetan schools, Mandarin is learned as the second language. In fact, some Tibetan parents do not want their kids to attend Tibetan schools. They would like their kids to attend Mandarin schools to have a mastery of fluent Mandarin because it would facilitate their kids' communication and work in areas outside of Tibet.

It is difficult to teach science subjects if all the teaching is done in Tibetan. Actually, mathematics, chemistry, and physics were taught with English terms in Chinese schools before the 1950s. Now we have introduced and set up adequate new words and terms for science subjects in Chinese. We once held an exhibition in Paris and presented textbooks both in Tibetan and Mandarin at the same time. A French visitor claimed that was really a wonderful practice, which couldn't be done in many countries due to the high cost of having two series of textbooks and two teams of teachers. In view of this, one cannot take learning Mandarin for assimilation. Tibetan parents ask their children to learn Mandarin, which is a similar case in big cities like Beijing and Shanghai, where parents ask their children to learn English.

John: You are telling us this now and that's great. But you haven't told the world this China's story about Tibet. We know this China's story about Tibet and we are persuaded by China's position, so we have it in our book *China's Megatrends*.

But here you have got the Dalai Lama issue. Actually Doris spoke to him in person some years ago. The Dalai Lama is not a giant intellect; he is quite cunning but he is not a big intellect. How can this man continuously outsmart the very smart Chinese? You know, you have a much better story. You ought to be smarter than the Dalai Lama. But how come every time, including this week, he outsmarts all of the Chinese? It's amazing. You've got to be really much more aggressive about China's story concerning Tibet. Or the Dalai Lama is going to continue outsmarting you every time.

Zhao: I think we need a self-examination of our PR work on Tibet and the way to convey the message on Tibet to the international community. Surely, there is room for further improvement in our work. As for the story of Tibet, we tend to believe that it's so clear-cut concerning what is wrong and what is right. However, people overseas may not have such a clear-cut picture about the fact. So I think we need to have a better understanding of this point. Since you are going to visit Tibet very soon, it will be a very important trip. During your stay in Tibet, you will have the opportunity to talk directly and informally with various people. I think after your visit, you may have some new and better suggestions for us, and we will be very happy to consider them.

In future discussions about the issues of Tibet, I think, in addition to official voice and press editorials, we should encourage more people from China and abroad, people like you, to participate. We need to carry out public diplomacy, not just government diplomacy so that we may be able to tell the story of Tibet in a more comprehensive and truthful manner.

Tibetans paying more attention to spiritual life

Doris: We have a very limited understanding of the whole situation in Tibet, but with our very limited understanding, we know there are two features: one is religion and the other spiritual orientation.

Before 1950, religion had a very strong position in Tibet. It means that 90 percent of the population were serving the monks and the feudal rulers. With the Chinese troops coming, they have lost their privileged positions, but 90 percent of the population has gained a much better position. Because they were gaining their rights, able to make their living, they would not be serfs any more. Therefore, many of the elite of the spiritual group went to Europe. Many of them are in Switzerland now, and they have made their voices heard very much. This is one feature.

The other feature is that, to our understanding, it was a very spiritual-oriented society. Tibetans have a more spiritual view on life than Han people or other ethnic groups in daily life. In general, Han people are more practical, more ambitious, so that gives them a big advantage and allows them to make economic progress faster, gaining a bigger share in the increasing wealth. The West takes this as an argument against Han people and even if some agree to certain positive facts on China, "yes-but" remains.

Zhao: It seems to me you have acquired a rich knowledge of Tibet rather than a limited understanding of it as you said. After your visit to Tibet, I think you'll become a full-fledged expert on Tibet (John and Doris all laugh). The practical life you mentioned means the material life in contrast with spiritual life. It is obvious that Tibetans' living standard has been greatly improved.

Western media often say that in 1950 the Chinese army occupied Tibet. Well, following their logic, I may continue saying that the PLA occupied lots of provinces and cities in China from 1947 to 1950, including Beijing, Shanghai, Hainan Island and all of China except Taiwan Province. From this perspective, it could be called "occupied," that is, there is no difference between occupying Beijing and occupying Tibet, because both of them are Chinese territory.

Doris: You should let the media know this!

Valuing the criterion for right and wrong

John: I think the West welcomes the Tibet issue to beat up on China, and up to now, this week and in the future, they always want to defeat China with Tibet, so you have to figure out how to really deal with that.

Doris: I want to add one more point. As for the president or the prime minister of any other country in the world, if they are going to meet the Dalai Lama tomorrow, they will not ask China for permission whether they can welcome the Dalai Lama or not. They will make a decision according to their own mind and judgment; and China should not intervene.

John: For example, when French President Sarkozy invited the Dalai Lama in 2008, the big story was that China tried to prevent it, you know, and reciprocated against France simply because they invited the Dalai Lama. When you do that, you make the Dalai Lama bigger and bigger and bigger and bigger, and, in fact, contribute to his image promotion. It might be better just to ignore him for a while. (Laughing)

Zhao: If the Chinese government did not officially lodge a definite protest against the reception of the Dalai Lama by the leader of some country, it would evoke strong repercussions among the Chinese people. They might say to Sarkozy that they would not buy French products or go to French supermarkets. They would wonder why China has bought so many Airbuses. If the Chinese government did not make any protest, people would make stronger reactions. So the Chinese government has expressed the collective will of the people. Overseas people may not fully understand it.

John: But you should notice that makes him only bigger and bigger.

Zhao: Actually, as the Dalai Lama is getting older and older, he becomes more and more arrogant. China's protest has made some countries think about the price they have to pay for the meeting with him and the way to receive him. Chinese put more emphasis on the distinction of what is right and what is wrong, while some Westerners under the pretense of "freedom" hold that whether they are going to meet the Dalai Lama or not is their freedom of choice and any third party should not interfere, thus covering up the distinction between right and wrong in the real essence of the issue. Our "interference" is intended to keep them from interfering with the basic interests of our country. Of the two kinds of interference, which one is more reasonable?

Doris: Then who defines the benchmark of right and wrong?

Zhao: Of course, the Chinese view on what is right or wrong should be taken as the criterion for China's affairs. Since China is the victim of instigation of Tibet for independence, China's power of voice should be respected. Actually, it is not necessary to analyze the conflict of the two views by elevating it to the one between the two world outlooks. You can see clearly what is right and what is wrong only by judging whether there is any interference with China's internal affairs.

Doris: There are many amazing war strategies or successful policies in Chinese history. As for the issue of the Dalai Lama, if you want your voice to be heard, you have to have better arguments and a better strategy.

Zhao: I'm sure you will have more updated and profound views on Tibet after your return from there.

John: We will share our views with you and the readers.

More about Tibet after a visit there

Zhao: It was 10 years ago when I visited Tibet for the first time.

When I got off the plane, I was deeply impressed by the blue sky and high mountains. What's your personal experience of this Tibet visit?

John: One of the places in China that fascinated us the most is Tibet. We certainly do not know enough to give a conclusive statement about Tibet, but we have met many different people and visited a number of places, so we have a very good first impression.

Zhao: The ceilings of five halls in the Potala Palace are covered by gold-plated bronze tiles, and they look glittering and imposing. If you do not observe them, you won't understand the essence of Tibetan ancient architectural art.

John: It is really true. They are marvelous. Besides the Potala Palace, we also visited the University of Tibet, the Tibet Autonomous Region Archive, the Lalu Wetland, and so on. Of course, we were impressed by the modernity of Tibet. We did not come without doing some research on Tibet. As you know, we dedicated a small chapter of our book to Tibet. At that time we had already been surprised about how little we knew and how distorted and single-edged the picture of Tibet was in the West.

Zhao: It has taken decades for the West to paint the distorted picture of Tibet, which disguises the Dalai Lama as a spiritual leader of the Tibetan people by covering up his separatist nature in politics, so that "the issue of the Dalai Lama" has been made into "the issue of Tibet" and been further internationalized. Without the support of international anti-China forces, the Dalai Lama would not have managed to be seen in such a light.

Doris: China is facing two strong spin doctors: the Dalai Lama and the movie *Seven Years in Tibet*. In addition, there is the picture the Tibetan exile government is painting: A land of monks, nuns and priests almost solely engaged in practicing their religion, ruled by a devout man without any striving for worldly power.

One cannot blame average people too much if they pick up on what is served to them on a silver platter while any better understanding about Tibet takes some digging. It starts by judging the landmass of Tibet. Most people think it is "very small but very important." Hardly anyone is aware of the real size. And all you see of Tibet in Western media are temples, monks, prostrating people, and Chinese soldiers with stern faces. With those pictures, how can the Western public question what the Dalai Lama says?

Zhao: After the "3/14 Incident" in Lhasa in 2008, most Western reports did not tell the truth and even intentionally grafted the picture of the lama riot on Nepalese streets on to the reports of the incident in Tibet. To ensure personal safety then, most foreign journalists were invited out of Tibet, and this resulted in the missing of an opportunity for them to witness the incident.

In an interview with former CBS anchor Dan Rather in February 2008, he asked me, "I had an interview with the Dalai Lama, and he said the Chinese government had suppressed religion in Tibet and damaged many religious institutions there. Is that true?"

I answered, "There were some such cases during the Cultural Revolution, but the situation has changed fundamentally. The Chinese government has not only restored temples, but also taken measures at great expense for their protection according to the cultural heritage protection standards. If I say today that Catholicism persecuted scientists, it should be pointed out that it happened in the 16th and 17th centuries, not now; nor should it be simply ascribed to Catholicism, but specifically to the Inquisition." Dan Rather agreed with me. I believe real mutual understanding can be achieved only through communication.

John: Exactly. But as Doris said, hardly anyone in the West is aware of that. In the 1960s, there was the New Age Movement① in the West. They were looking for alternative lifestyles, and they were very much influenced by the gurus in India as well as the Dalai Lama. They looked for enlightenment; some even took a journey to Tibet and deified the Dalai Lama.

Some Hollywood stars like Richard Gere② hail the Dalai Lama, and this in part makes the Dalai Lama a global figure.

Zhao: At the annual "Sino-German Forum," a famous industrial leader in Germany also mentioned this. He said some Europeans even see the Dalai Lama as being greater than the Pope. This surprised me a lot, and also made me realize how his religious cloak conceals his political ambition.

I wonder if you have watched or heard about *A Year in Tibet*. This documentary was not produced by Chinese. In order to make this

---

① The New Age Movement emerged in the 1960s and developed in the following decades. It started in Western Europe and North America and then swept the whole world. Advocating the search for cultural roots, it created a global anti-modernity trend. It had a great impact on academia, ideology, religion, science, law, business, literature, arts and daily life.

② Richard Tiffany Gere, a famous Hollywood star, is best known for his leading role in *American Gigolo*, *An Officer and a Gentleman*, and *Pretty Woman*. He was winner of the Golden Globe Award for the Best Performance by an Actor in a Motion Picture-Comedy or Musical.

movie, a production unit of BBC spent a year in Tibet, where they interviewed Tibetans and tracked their real life.

In early March 2008, just a few days after BBC aired the first episode, the "3/14 Incident" took place. Thus the movie attracted more attention in the West.

The movie was attacked by the "Free Tibet" organization. After watching the advance notice on the day before the first episode was aired, they said that the movie "beautified" the Chinese government, and "BBC had fallen into the trap of the Chinese government."

A spokesperson for BBC said that as an observational documentary, *A Year in Tibet* was intended for people to learn more about the daily life of real Tibetans at that time, not for a detailed analysis of Tibetan history or politics.

If some Western writers—at present they are still a small number—are those ghost drivers you mentioned earlier, their presenting the real Tibet to the Western public may be regarded by Tibetan separatist organizations and some Western media as "falling into the trap of the Chinese government." It is indeed lamentable to disallow honest people to tell the truth.

Doris: Absolutely. But of course you cannot bring everybody to Tibet. So what is needed is a balanced reporting. I would like to come back to the article in *Stern*. In my memory, it was the first article for a long time that questioned the myth that people in Tibet had lived in paradise before the Han people returned to it. The article was entitled "The Dalai Lama is not an innocent angel." It pointed out that Tibet had not been a paradise at all but run as a theocracy with

95 percent of the people being serfs and not allowed to learn how to read or write.

Zhao: There are quite a lot of studies and reports about the misery of serfs in the old Tibet. They were deprived of basic human rights, and the slave owners and the Dalai Lama used religion to tame the serfs and make them prostrate before their fate and accept the status of being enslaved. The situation lasted till the 1950s.

You have been to Tibet, traveled a lot of places and talked with many people. Perhaps you have noticed some remains of the old Tibet.

John: When we were in Lhasa, we did not only visit the wonderful rooms of Potala Palace, but also saw the jail where disobedient serfs had been tortured. Doris asked the guide, an old man who had served in Potala Palace when the Dalai Lama had been there, whether the Dalai Lama had known that a hundred meters below his rooms, the eyes of serfs were burned out with boiling oil, hands cut off, or whatever other horrible punishment was carried out in such cases. "Yes," he said, after hesitating awhile, "but you know, the Dalai Lama was very young. "

Zhao: When I was studying in Beijing at the end of the 1950s, I visited an exhibition about Tibet, where I saw shanks and skulls cut off from serfs and used as musical instruments and other apparatuses for religious ceremonies. They still remain fresh in my memory today. There are several kinds of serfdoms in the world, but the cruelty of the one in old Tibet was unparalleled. When the Dalai Lama was enthroned in 1939, he was only four years old, so he should not be held accountable for the serfdom and the alliance between politics and religion. From 1954 to 1956, he had close cooperation with the Chinese Central Government. However, in the subsequent decades, he cannot escape the responsibility for the offense of attempting to split China.

John: So on the one hand we see the Dalai Lama's glorification of Tibet's history and condemnation of the Chinese, and on the other hand we have a very unskillful handling of the Dalai Lama's very skillful anti-China campaign. As you have said before, Mr. Zhao, China has to improve its handling of press matters. To the " official China" the Dalai Lama is like a red flag in a Spanish bullfight. You wave it and the bull comes running. Every time the Dalai Lama is received by any Western politician, China comes running and fuming, and many people in the world blame China for being aggressive against this "man of peace." It is a trap in which China steps, and it is working for the Dalai Lama every time.

Zhao: As for some Western leaders' meetings with the Dalai Lama, the Chinese government must protest them, because they infringe upon China's core interests. Although those Western political leaders insist on such meetings, they have to carefully handle and reduce the impact of such meetings. Otherwise, they have to pay a price for offending China. The Dalai Lama is cheating the innocent and kind-hearted people across the world with his smiles and lies. We only want people to know what is behind his smiles. "Dalai: Your smiles charm but your actions harm." This is a slogan opposing the Dalai Lama's visit to the United States on a streamer hanging from an airplane above Seattle, in the United States, before the Beijing Olympics.

Doris: As said before, we would like to know what would happen if he were ignored by China. It always needs two parties, one that acts and the other that reacts. I wonder if China can take the acting part, and have a sort of image campaign on Tibet. If the people's picture about Tibet is correct, then their opinion about the Dalai Lama and what he says will be based on that picture. As long as he can appear as "the savior of Tibet," nothing will change. It is not easy because who would be against peace and harmony, which the Dalai Lama preaches. That way he has gained a lot of moral authority in the world. But I have never heard an interview where the journalist was really tough on the reality of Tibet's past. They think it is kind of a sacrilege to touch anything that contradicts what he says.

Zhao: You said that people should have a realistic picture of Tibet in their minds. This is really what we have to do further. Only if we tell the true story of Tibet can people disbelieve those false stories about Tibet.

Doris: Last time I mentioned Fareed Zakaria's interview with the Dalai Lama. Zakaria challenged the Dalai Lama's claim that Tibet should go back to the Tibetans by asking the latter to define the size of the so called "Greater Tibet." It was a tough question to the Dalai Lama and he was circling around it without a definite answer. What has been claimed by the Dalai Lama is about 25 percent of China's territory. So Zakaria let him go as he had done with some other matters. If somebody on that occasion says, "OK, let's put the things on the table: What is the territory you claim and why do you do it?" I think he would stand on pretty weak ground.

Zhao: An American media mogul once said that the 14th Dalai in essence is "a very political old monk shuffling around in Gucci shoes." Some Western commentaries also said that the Dalai Lama often achieves his "PR success." The Dalai Lama is really slick and sly, but we cannot counter his moves in the same way. However, besides governmental diplomacy, it is also necessary for us to step up public diplomatic efforts.

John: We should talk about Tibet and not get stuck on the Dalai Lama. What impressed us a lot was how much China is pushing for a better education of the Tibetan population. But not only that, Tibetan culture seems to be very much in the center of interest. We have visited the University of Tibet, and we visited several primary schools, including a school in the countryside. This particular school had not been in the plan of our visits, so we were sure this was not a model school. We were very impressed by the standards we saw.

Zhao: Before the peaceful liberation of Tibet in the 1950s, all of Tibet had no single regular school in the modern sense, and there were only schools run by temples and the Tibetan local government for monk officials and children of the nobility. At that time, the enrollment rate of school-age children in Tibet was less than 2 percent, and the illiteracy rate among the young and the adults aged 30-50 was as high as 95 percent.

Two decades ago, the Chinese government started compulsory education with free food and free accommodations in Tibet. Schooling was no longer a family burden. Kids did not have to bring anything and could go to school by simply taking with them a toothbrush and toothpaste. At the end of 2007, the primary school enrollment rate had reached 98. 2 percent, secondary school enrollment rate 90. 8 percent, and illiteracy among the young and the adults aged 30-50 had been basically eliminated. Education in Tibet is entering the best and fastest period of development in history.

Doris: We were impressed by cell phones and computers programmed in the Tibetan language, because we heard that the language is not exactly matching that challenge.

Zhao: That's true. It took more than 10 years to adapt the Chinese language to digital technology, including accurately establishing thousands of professional terms and the Chinese character input method. However, the Tibetan language is able to adapt to the development of digital technology more quickly with the Chinese language as the bridge. While developing the modern Tibetan language, the government also has made a herculean effort to protect the Tibetan writing and language, and the Tibetan Autonomous Region has issued regulations and rules on learning to use and develop the Tibetan language and literature, thus providing legal guarantees in this regard. In order to promote the Tibetan language and literature, local governments have compiled five sets of Tibetan textbooks, including students' books, syllabuses and teachers' books from the primary school to the university.

John: What you are telling us now and what we saw with our own eyes is great. But it does not help to correct the picture of Tibet if only a few people in the West know it. Whatever we knew at the time, we have put in our book *China's Megatrends.* We know we will go back to learn more about Tibet.

Zhao: I welcome you to visit there again, and hope I myself will have more chances to go there as well. If possible, we may go there by train so as to have an objective understanding of the situation along the Qinghai-Tibet Railway. I'm sure we will have many new experiences.

John: It's a good idea to go there by train. We hope we'll have more chances to visit Tibet, too.

Part Four

On Science, Education and Intellectual Property

Lagging behind in science and technology

John: Concerning the development of science, I would like to ask Mr. Zhao, why did China fall so behind while Western countries were advancing scientifically? What happened?

Zhao: China has a very long history as a feudal society. During that period, the imperial examination system, an important system in Chinese feudal society, was set up. Its advantage was to open the door to officialdom for all Chinese intellectuals. Anyone, no matter what his background, could enjoy the opportunity to become an official if he could pass the examinations. Examinees had to be good at writing and the theory of governance. They were even required to be good at poetry, rhyme prose and calligraphy. In order to pass the examinations, the examinees had to spend a lot of time preparing, normally 10 to 20 years. Therefore, they could not concentrate their time and energy on developing science and technology. Neither was there enough drive in them to pursue that goal.

This may be one of the causes. Of course there are others. I would like to know your bystanders' view.

John: When you examine a society or a country, you always ask two questions. What is rewarded in the society? And what is punished? The former means what reward would one get if one works diligently. The latter means what punishment would one get if one has done something wrong. No matter what you talk about, be it a family or institution or society or the whole country, if you find answers to the above questions, you'll get a lot of information about that society.

Zhao: A tenet in Chinese history was "Excellence in learning would help one become an official." If one were good at learning how to pass the imperial examination, one would have the opportunity to become an official. That was a big reward and attraction for Chinese intellectuals. There were not many options in an agricultural society, and being an official was the best option for a scholar to stand out among his peers, enjoy a high social status and earn a high salary. Ancient Chinese looked down upon merchants, who could not be compared with scholars in status. Therefore, Chinese have constantly underrated commerce. As for industry in ancient China, there was only cottage industry with handwork technology without any large factories due to the small-scale peasant economy and backward transportation. The underdevelopment of a commercial market, in turn, resulted in the underdevelopment of a technological market. There was no drive for people to work on technological innovation.

John: Perhaps now we should focus upon China today. We should ask the same questions: "What is rewarded and what is punished in today's China?"

Zhao: Concerning the rewards for technological contributions, you may know that since the reform and opening up, the government has issued many kinds of yearly rewards divided into different levels to winners for their achievements in science and technology, including basic science and technological application. Personally, I was also awarded local and national prizes for inventions in new technology.

In 2006, China issued the National Program for Mid- and Long-term Development of Science and Technology as its national strategy, which proposed the supportive policies, goals and development of investment in the future.

We cannot catch up with advanced countries in all fields overnight. However, we should have our priorities, encourage innovations by Chinese scientists, and make efforts to convert scientific achievements into commercial products.

John: You are saying that the government has issued rewards for scientific research and innovation. But I'm more interested in how the society makes evaluations. You have mentioned that in the feudal period the society didn't value merchants very well. What does the society value today? That is what the society rewards. What do the people value in the society? What do they value people doing? What are they negative about?

Zhao: In China, the best benchmark is the selection of majors by college entrance examination takers. Two areas are most popular among them: one relating to finance and law, which were not stressed before the reform and opening up of China, and the other relating to advanced branches of science, including physics, biochemistry and mathematics, which would be selected by the best students.

John: Yes, exactly.

Zhao: Among those students studying in European countries or the United States, the majority study natural sciences and modern technologies. There are two reasons. One is their preference for those majors and the other is that the tuition for those majors is far less than that for medicine, law or finance. Perhaps it is due to the unwillingness of American students to select majors in science and technology that gives opportunities to overseas Chinese students.

Placing high priority on innovation in science and technology

Doris: I'd like to come back to the question about science. You have talked about what was in the feudal system and what was convenient to the ruling class when education was in the hands of few. In Europe, for many centuries, education was in the hands of the Catholic Church. Scientific research and scientific progress were made against the will of the Catholic Church, and many scientists throughout history suffered constraints and punishments. Scientific progress went hand in hand with a breakthrough against the power of the Catholic Church, which then had to change and adapt to the new conditions. When you have breakthroughs, you always have a break with existing rules. That's in the nature of breakthroughs. The question is: How free is the Chinese society and how much does it support breakthroughs?

Zhao: In China we do not have any constraints like those in the times of Copernicus on breakthroughs in scientific research. When people are not worried about their survival, they are driven by endless curiosity and imagination, which promote the development of science. According to Albert Einstein, imagination is more important than knowledge. Traditional Chinese education emphasized the accumulation of knowledge and neglected the cultivation of imagination and innovation. Therefore, first of all, Chinese scientists and technologists should heighten their awareness of innovation. For example, when a scientist has imagined something feasible, whether he can put it into further practice depends on the availability of a team, laboratory, and funds. Such material constraints are ubiquitous; and with the increase of national strength, the Chinese government's support for scientific research goes up year by year.

Just now you have mentioned the influence of the Catholic Church in the Middle Ages on science, and it reminds me of a story of our time. Several years ago, President George W. Bush suddenly declared that the U. S. government would stop any official support for stem cell research. It was said that the research conflicted with his Christian belief. But in the eyes of many scientists, the study of stem cells is very useful for patients, because it can lead to the stage of making artificial organs to save many patients in the future. Now President Obama has restored federal support for the study of stem cells. The flip-flop is very interesting, for it demonstrates the effect of a given belief on the thinking of a state leader. For any person, it is very difficult to separate his/her thinking and even judgment from the creed of his/her belief.

John: I think your point is well-made and I want to add a little bit. In the United States, the funds for stem cell research actually come from individual states and some private companies, which contribute the majority of the funds, while the federal government contributes only a small part. What Bush banned was the federal money. Moreover, Bush is a Protestant rather than a Catholic. My question is that in your view how to make the distinction between theoretical research and applied research.

Zhao: I can answer your questions only from the perspective of physics, and in some areas the distinction between the two is blurred. The aim of physical research is to explore the properties and laws of nature, for example, the structures, the law of movement and the interaction of various kinds of materials. Sometimes the results of theoretical research cannot be verified at once and further experiments are needed. An example in point is the research result achieved by Dr. Li Zhengdao (Tsung-dao Lee) and Dr. Yang Zhenning (Chenning Franklin Yang). Only until Dr. Wu Jianxiong (Chien-shiung Wu) verified their theory later through a fabulous experiment did they get the Nobel Prize. However, theoretical research cannot necessarily be put into immediate practice; sometimes it takes applied research to transform it into practical technology. For example, Einstein's theory of $E = mc^2$ was put forward in 1905 and resulted in the emergence of nuclear reactors and nuclear bombs through applied research some 40 years later in the 1940s.

Theoretical researchers work hard, and their achievements are not easily applied in time. Only those who aspire to make great scientific achievements can learn the theories of science. I personally have learned experimental physics, and I'm not that kind of person who is very talented in theory.

No taboo subjects in academic discussions in China

Doris: Back to the story of Albert Einstein. Would Einstein with his rebellious character have succeeded in China? When I made an analogy of the Roman Catholic Church, it was because more often than not, talented people hold some rebellious views which might be incompatible with the views of such a system. If some scientifically talented people in China—without any political attempts—argue for something which would not be conformable to the present system, would they get support from the society?

Zhao: Inheriting the traditions in a critical way means criticizing what one believes is wrong while inheriting what one thinks is right and developing new ideas. This is actually a driving force for social progress. In China there are no taboo subjects in academic discussions. Scientific issues cannot be resolved by democratic means or voting to determine whether they are true or false. New theories of science are often understood only by a small number of people in the beginning. If issues are related to the political system, democracy will be required and their solutions will need to be determined by the will of the majority of people. It is one thing to put forward counter-mainstream views from research on political issues, and it is another to conduct political activities for the purposes of overthrowing the government and the constitution, because the constitution has been determined through democratic procedure.

John: Albert Einstein often quarreled with his colleagues or other physicists. In fact, criticisms and quarrels between colleagues and counterparts are significant to technological development. We know in China there is no colleague criticism, and a peer review of scientific papers is almost a sweetheart one. It's not easy to exchange criticism on scientific papers; however, this is necessary to get the juices going for breakthroughs in science. Is it changing? Scientists and academics are quite critical, and everyone who does not criticize each other does not advance very well.

Zhao: Indeed, some talented people are eccentric, like Picasso, a contemporary of Albert Einstein. The former painted pictures with space disorder that people then could not understand; for example, his *Les Demoiselles d'Avignon*, which I cannot understand even today. The latter put forward the surprising new theory on the concept of time and space. However, they both made absolute contributions to world civilization.

About competition in Chinese scientific circles

Zhao: I acknowledge that there exists such a glaring defect in the Chinese academic circle as you pointed out just now. Sometimes Chinese would like to live in harmony in a small environment. Albert Einstein was a theoretical physicist and didn't need an assistant, so he could still achieve success even with such a bad temper. If he had been an experimental physicist, he would have been doomed to failure.

John: You bet!

Zhao: Nowadays, if we want to set up a large-scale accelerator, we need several hundred people for its design. If the team leader cannot work together with other people, the project will not succeed. The point can be illustrated with the example of the Manhattan Project. Had Dr. Oppenheimer been such an eccentric and unsociable man, he would not have become "Father of the Atomic Bomb." It was fortunate that Einstein was a theoretical scientist, not an experimental physicist, and Picasso needed no assistant. Thus it did not matter for him to have a bad temper.

John: Absolutely.

Doris: Coming back to the topic of China's technological system. China's scientific circle has an underdeveloped competitive environment. Why is that? To our understanding the answer can be best seen from a cultural perspective. Failure is not really welcome in Chinese society because it makes you lose face. Once you have lost face, it's very hard to come back. It is different in Western society, especially in American society, where if you fail, you get yourself together and try even harder to come back without feeling the loss of face. This is part of the secret to success in American society. You can try and err on a large scale in China, but on a personal scale, you fail and that's not very good.

John: Billy Wilder① once said, "Success means to stand up one more time."

Zhao: Thank you for sharp criticism. Without criticism between scientists, there would be no drive for them to improve an initial achievement. Sometimes, it may give rise to pseudoscience. Of course, pseudoscience will go bust one day; however, during its existence, it hampers the development of science.

Seeing talent as a global commodity

Zhao: After the discussion on science, we should move on to the topic of education.

John: Great! We are very interested in education and what your view is on that topic. Today in the global market our economies are growing interdependent and we are moving toward one market and one economy for the whole world. This also leads to one market for talent, no country can isolate itself. The question is which country possesses the most prosperous talent pool and that country can hope to

---

① Billy Wilder (1906 – 2002) was an American screenwriter and film director with his career spanning more than 50 years and 60 films, including *Double Indemnity*, *The Lost Weekend*, and *Sunset Boulevard*.

grasp the biggest share in the global market. As you have written in your book *Pudong Miracle*, [1] "Those who have the talented people will command the heights. " In this sense, either in Eastern countries or Western countries, what we really have to fight for is the talent, which has become a global commodity. And, as you wrote, he who has the best people will command the heights.

Doris: The question also is, "How and why could America command the heights for such a long time?" What worries the West is that if China combines the talent it possesses simply by its population with an education reform enforced with the efficiency of its vertical democracy, how long will it take China to overtake the global market with technological advances?

Zhao: You have talked about the issue of talent that both of us are interested in. Now the number of talents in China is several times that of 30 years ago. But the percentage of scientists, technicians and artists among the population is still quite lower than that of the developed countries. That's why we set the policy of "promoting the country's development through science and education. " I strongly believe that science will not develop if education is not improved. So I am more concerned about educational reform. Education is an issue relating to all Chinese families. It is a tradition in China that children's education is the priority of the family. Parents may reduce costs in various expenses, and it does not matter if their clothing and housing are poor, but they will try their best to send their children to good schools and give their children all-out support. I think that is a

---

[1]   Zhao Qizheng and Shao Yudong, *Shanghai Pudong Miracle* (China Intercontinental Press, July 2008). It is a record of the process of Pudong development and also a collection of important concepts and views gradually formed in practice by all the previous municipal party committees, municipal governments and people who took part in the development of Pudong.

very good foundation for the development of education in China. Even so, the education of China is still behind that of the Western countries, particularly in terms of excellent universities, the number of which is much fewer in China than that in Europe, the United States and Japan. Our teaching methods still need further improvement.

Bringing reform to Chinese education

John: Well, I think in our conversation in February 2009, in Beijing, we agreed that the No. 1 priority for China, indeed the No. 1 priority for any country in the coming world we live in, is education, even from an economic perspective. Now China is starting to talk about the use of the independent classroom, talking about educational reform. But you know no country has got an educational system that suits the new world, the new integrated global world where innovation is so important to all. The world today is increasingly dependent and innovative. The complaining in China is that everything you teach is for the examinations, and you award teachers by how well the students do in the examinations. That's actually more or less true of all countries in the world. Look at France. At any time during the school hours, every school child in the same grade is doing exactly the same thing. Teaching through the exams! It's an opportunity as long as you are going to reform the educational system. Why not really reform it and lead the world in creating an educational system for the 21st century?

Zhao: As I have already said, the disadvantage of China's exam system has its historical roots. China has a very long history of imperial examinations, starting in the Sui Dynasty about 1,400 years ago and continuing to the end of the Qing Dynasty in 1911. All the scholars had to go through those examinations if they wanted to become officials in the government. The examinees had to be very good at quoting the classics in their papers. To do so, they had to spend a lot of time in rote learning. Therefore, the option for the intellectuals then was to have a good mastery of literature. They also had to be able to talk eloquently about the strategy for making the country prosperous. The advantage of this system was that average people had the opportunity to go through the examinations in order to become officials in the government, unlike the hereditary system for nobility in Europe. Now science subjects weigh heavy in our secondary education. Even the college math course for freshmen in Europe and the U. S. is taught in Chinese high schools. However, classroom teaching still focuses on the input of knowledge and overlooks the development of innovative mentality. We have to change this tradition. But it's not so easy. First, we should have excellent teachers who can inspire innovation among students. Then, I think besides increasing the budget for education, we should advocate a "classroom revolution," that is, we should reform teaching methods to enable the development of students' innovative ability.

Doris: I disagree with you that China has fewer talents than the rest of the world. I really feel that China has as much talent as, or may be even more talent, certainly in absolute figures, than the rest of the world. But what we have seen in looking at China and into its educational system is that China obviously wastes a lot of talent. If we consider the huge number of migrant workers in the *hukou* (household registration) system, whose children do not have equal access to education then we seem to have a cat that bites its own tail. If the migrant worker comes, for example, from some little village in western China to Beijing and he takes his child with him, he cannot afford a decent schooling. If he leaves his child in the village with his parents, the school does not have the level of the Beijing school. So to us, this system is totally not understandable, especially if the political system is otherwise so efficient. Can this be changed in a much faster way than it is done?

Zhao: Right now, the *hukou* system is undergoing reform. If you look at the Chinese population, the urban population accounts for about 45 percent of the total population, while the rural population accounts for about 55 percent. So there is still a long way to go for urbanization in China, and the task cannot be accomplished in a short period of time but carried out step by step. In the past few years, the annual increase of urban population in China has been about 1 percent. In fact the control of household registration has loosened very much. For example, there are 18 million people in Shanghai, including locals and long-term residents without household registration. Of them, about 13.5 million have registered permanent residences in Shanghai and 4.5 million haven't, excluding short-term residents that cannot be properly categorized. In the case of Beijing, altogether there are about 17 million permanent residents. Of them, 5.09 million have no registered permanent residences in Beijing.

Now many cities have put forward plans to solve the education problem for children of migrant workers and try their best to make local education available to them.

John: In China, "migrant workers" means the surplus rural labor power that flowed into the cities. In the West, for example, in the United States, migrant workers are mostly from Mexico during the seasons of harvest, the corn harvest or apple harvest, before they go back to Mexico. It's a seasonal thing. And of course migrant workers here are hundreds of millions of people from the farms who came to the cities and work as factory workers, construction workers, household workers and so on. Of course, the migrant workers' consideration in China is huge.

Doris mentioned innovation and there is a reason that there is so much talking about innovation in the world today. And that's because given the kind of world we live in, we have to innovate even to keep pace with ourselves. I was very impressed by what President Hu Jintao said at the 17th National Congress of the Communist Party of China in 2007. Now in the West a lot of companies and executives give good service in innovation, and they may conceive that you have just passed a law and say, "OK, from now on, all companies and executives are going to be innovative." Judging from what President Hu said, I think it is clear that he understands that you can't order this, and you can't pass laws saying you have to have innovation. What you have to do, or the government's role, is to create a nourishing environment in which innovation can flower—the environment which we know is necessary for innovation, even though we never know where it's coming from. So the strategy is creating a nourishing environment. And that applies to education.

Concerning education, of course, we should learn literature, language and history. And I believe we should promote innovative spirits even among primary school students, to have a nourishing environment for people to start to recognize that they have talent and start to think what they are going to contribute to this very society on their own, and that's all we have to think about. However, either in China or in other countries, education is rigid, without innovative spirits. We send our children every day to schools, but it is not a nourishing environment. It is rigid all over the world. It's terrible.

Introducing competition into education

John: Here I would like to offer my personal views on educational reform. I just refer to higher education in the United States, excluding the middle school and the primary school. The American education system is probably the best in the world, because it has a competitive mechanism.

In our book *China's Megatrends* we focused on eight main pillars. If we would add a ninth pillar, it would be competition. One of the pillars for China's great success is competition. It's not known very much in the West that competition has been so important to the advancement of China: competition among the provinces, among cities, among companies. Now we need competition in education. If you want to change your educational system quickly, the only one way to achieve it is competition. The U. S. clearly has the best system of higher education, not primary education but higher education, in the world. Why? Because of competition. The U. S. has about 4,500 colleges and universities, 40 percent of them private and 60 percent state. Virtually no national universities. The point is for decades all these colleges or universities have been in fierce competition to get students, to get customers. It's competition that gets the very best talents into your schools and, in turn, they increase the value of those institutions.

Zhao: There is competition in China's college admission. We have about three or four tiers of universities, ranking from the national key universities (more than 50) like Tsinghua or Peking through provincially or municipally prestigious universities down to general or even poor-performing colleges. The best universities attract the best students, while in those less prestigious universities students find it hard to be employed after graduation. Actually it's the same in American universities. The graduates of Harvard, Yale and Stanford can easily find jobs, and it can be difficult for the graduates of those not-so-famous universities to find jobs. There are about 1, 000 universities and some private colleges in China. Most of the private colleges usually experience budget difficulties and teacher shortage, and they are weak in competition.

In China the educational budget is less than 4 percent of its GDP, while in the United States it is 7. 5 percent against the world average of 5 percent. So we have not yet invested enough into education and need to improve it.

John: I think we agree that America has the best higher education system because of competition. But competition is not limited to universities. It is more important to introduce competition into primary and middle schools. The competition among schools helps get students to come to good schools and keep moving the schools, and the parents decide which schools their kids go to depending on how good they are. This is a very radical thing to do, but it's the only way you can change a school very quickly. If you have schools compete to get customers, or compete to get students, you will apply to education what you've learned from the market economy. And you know this so well in the market economy about getting customers. The same ideas can be used to build your school for children, and have it competitive and getting better and better so that they will come to your school. A very good way to work that out. But in general the idea is competition among all schools, especially schools for the children.

Zhao: But in China, most of the schools, prestigious or not, are state-funded. If there were more private schools, your suggestion might be more effective.

A small number of private schools with high tuition fees in primary or secondary education have emerged in some cities of China. They often can hire good teachers because they are able to offer high salaries. They even hire overseas teachers to teach foreign languages. Then another problem arises, that is , only the rich can send their children to such private schools. So people call them aristocratic schools, and they create repugnance among many ordinary parents. This is a new problem.

John: In my example about higher education in the U. S. , 60 percent of the schools of higher education are state (provincial) government schools; only 40 percent are private schools. The government gives money to the schools that attract the most students. If it is not a very good school and people don't want to send their children to it and there are only a few students, it won't get very much budget from the state. But if schools are really good and lots of children want to come, they get very much budget from the state. There are ways to work it out. If you are not going to change, you will not get any educational reform of any substance at any time without competition.

Doris: Can Chinese parents choose schools for their children? I wonder whether China will include the freedom of choosing schools into its education reform.

Zhao: Concerning the freedom of choosing schools, one can choose any university regardless of the geographical restrictions. A student in Guangdong can apply for a university in Beijing and a student in

Beijing can apply for a university in Shanghai. There are no restrictions for them. The problem lies in primary schools and middle schools. For example, it seems not necessary for primary and middle school students in Shanghai to go to school in Beijing because there are good schools in Shanghai. And it is almost impossible for rural students to leave their parents for schooling in cities, since their families are not able to afford their tuitions and living expenses in cities. At the thought of their living away from home, their parents may also worry about their safety. So I think the priority is still to run rural schools well.

John: Yes. That's absolutely true.

Doris: I think another problem is updating the mindset. Teachers are the key to shape tomorrow's talent. However, yesterday's people are determining the education of tomorrow, because every teacher, of course, has the education of yesterday with the old mindset, but he/she should teach the children the new mindset, and I think that's very hard to overcome. How can you encourage the teachers to teach the necessities of tomorrow when teachers themselves have been taught the necessities of yesterday?

Zhao: In China we have a saying like this, "It takes 10 years to plant a tree, but it takes 100 years to educate a person." Why? Because it takes time to train good teachers before they foster good students. A good school results from the efforts of several generations of good teachers. So it takes a lot of years to educate a person when the time for teacher training is also included. We hope that teachers will keep in contact with society, keep abreast of the times, be aware of developing circumstances of society, gain knowledge at the frontiers of science and technology, and know what the enterprises are doing.

Some American corporations, such as AT&T and Intel, are not only manufacturers but also leaders in technological development. Exchanges between these companies and colleges on talent and information enable the development of universities. As dean of the School of Journalism, Renmin University of China, I deeply feel the complementary effect of the exchanges between me and professors. It would be a good method for one to think in the shoes of the other if there were a job exchange between a teacher and an official, or an engineer or a man of literature or an artist. But it is not easy, because it is a great challenge to change a career in one's life.

John: We both agree that education is the No. 1 priority for China. You just mentioned that competition might not be an effective way. Then what do you think should China do to reform its education system?

Zhao: I did not mean to oppose the introduction of competition into the reform of education as you suggested, but my concern is that overemphasis on competition would undermine the demand for government funds, thus taking a school for an enterprise. The central and local governments should provide enough funds and support for both compulsory (elementary and middle schools) and noncompulsory (high school and college) education. Against such a background, we should make an all-around and effective plan to attract funds through competition and provide scholarships for those poverty-stricken students. As I just mentioned, all educational reforms should not neglect the reform of teaching methods. This is a reform that requires the participation of tens of thousands of teachers.

John: I have something to add. I was assistant to the Secretary of Education in the United States under President Kennedy, when I was only 33 years old. Since I was very interested in education, I later created the high school in Chicago called the "school without walls." I think we've just got to do something in all the countries in the world about education. We have to nourish our children. You know children are such great learners. We have grandchildren who are simultaneously learning two or three languages, and we know children who could learn three languages at two, three or four years old, so they are great learners. Then what do we do? We put them into schools and we slow them down to one step and then the next step and the next step. It's so boring. When we really do all this stuff, it is really crazy. As we just said, we need an educational reform to put our children's potential into full swing.

Zhao: In this sense, Americans need a "classroom revolution." Talents cultivated in the schools are the basis for scientific and technological development, and intellectual property rights (IPR) protection is also a necessity for the cultivation of talents. What's your view on that?

China already on the way to IPR protection

John: Concerning IPR protection, you can't solve intellectual problems by passing legislation, by passing a law saying "Please don't do it." The only way you can change the situation is in the marketplace. I remember years ago when I first came out with *Megatrends*, I could see all different versions of the book in Taiwan because it had more intellectual pirates than anywhere else in the world at that time. Then what happened was over the years Taiwan has started to develop its own intellectual properties. For IPR protection, they have enacted very tough laws, which apply to everybody. So over a period of time, Taiwan has become a place with almost no intellectual pirates any more. On the mainland, there are more intellectual properties developed both in books and in inventions, in software and hardware. So the more they are created by Chinese citizens, the more they have strong laws, which apply to everybody, to protect the intellectual properties for Chinese citizens, and the more you move to the other side where intellectual properties are very much protected. That's the path you are on. You are perhaps only half way, but that's the way you are going. I think in time it will take care of itself in the marketplace.

Zhao: You are right. When a country has its own intellectual properties in the form of new knowledge, books and inventions, it will pay much more attention to IPR protection. China is on its way to IPR protection. China declared the National IPR Strategic Program in June 2008, pointing out the direction for the strategy of IPR protection and proposing the establishment of the system for IPR protection nationwide.

I would like to tell you that the first and also the only IPR court that has existed for more than a decade was set up in Pudong New Area when I worked there. At that time, we found that IPR cases related to the civil, criminal, and administrative courts. Therefore, an IPR case was tried by three courts and penalized in different aspects. This gave rise to low efficiency and very often to conflicts. Therefore, the IPR court was set up in Pudong New Area at the beginning of 1996. It was called the "IPR Pudong Model" online. China is thinking about setting up courts like it nationwide. This is the latest news. I'm really proud that it is already 13 years since the IPR court in Pudong New Area was set up.

Doris: This also resulted from the high-speed development of Pudong, but you have some headwinds.

Zhao: Yes. Some people may complain that I have driven too fast, and those people investigated by the court, of course, are not satisfied either.

Doris: Let me use a metaphor. There is an apprentice to a great chef who has many secret recipes. And the apprentice is good at learning and learns fast. When he comes home, he does the same cooking at home. This is a different way of importing knowledge.

Zhao: Can the chef say that the apprentice has pirated his recipes? Maybe they can be counted as knowhow.

Doris: That's good to the customers, and they can get a taste of new cuisine. But it is unfair to the chef.

Zhao: Personally, I have three patents of my own or in collaboration with others, and I have written seven or eight books. So I have strong awareness of IPR protection.

John: Since we are co-working on this book, we should join our efforts in IPR protection.

Zhao: Maybe in the future I can help you to protect your books. On Sundays I may go to the bookstores to see if there are any pirated copies of your books; if there are, I may help you file a lawsuit in China.

John: Great!

Zhao: Good! (The two shake hands). Ah, this is a book coauthored by the three of us, so we three should shake hands. (The three shake hands.)

Now China has drawn up the mid- and long-term program for the development of science and technology. And there is a guard for this strategy: the IPR protection laws.

Handling IP piracy cases

Zhao: Recently, there was a well-known website case, "Tomato Garden." A small Chinese company pirated the Windows XP operating system and made some small changes to it. Then they sold the pirated copies online. The case was handled seriously by the Chinese court. The company was fined more than RMB ¥9 million, that is, more than US $1 million. The four defendants were sentenced to prison terms varying from six months to three years. Have you heard of that? It happened this year.

Doris: It's very good if that happens. But it also has to be transparent to the West. The West needs to know that. Whether it is aviation, automobiles or other technologies, the Western opinion is that China "imports" knowledge through the back door. I think one has to really assure Western companies they can expect to be safe with their technologies. Now the picture is that you come and have a joint venture for three years, and then you are out of the market, but a copy of your product is in the market.

Zhao: When I was head of Pudong New Area, I handled some cases like this. The first case was in 1995 and it involved the copying and pirating of the Gillette shaver technology. We handled the case seriously and severely fined the IP pirates. During the investigation, we found there were multiple causes for piratical cases. Sometimes the employees, including both Chinese and foreigners, were not loyal to their company. However, the Chinese government understands that if such practice is tolerated, it will reduce the investment and high-tech transfer by high-tech companies in China. So the Chinese government is very resolute on IPR protection and firmly against the piracy of intellectual properties.

John: These are very good cases.

Zhao: With regard to a lawsuit filed by a Western company about its IPR infringement, the IPR court will sentence the pirates to make compensations for the damage according to the law. Those cases have been reported more or less in some Western media.

Doris: As China is very strongly decentralizing, a lot of investment directly goes into the provinces. While it is pretty obvious the interest of the government is to protect intellectual properties, the temptation to go the easy way might be stronger in places where the "emperor" is far away.

We were very impressed by what you did in Pudong and the measures you put up against the corruption, including the firewall. ① But other cities and provinces might not do so well.

---

① It refers to a measure taken by the Management Committee of Pudong New Area to prevent government officials from gaining personal interests with power; there are three such firewalls or measures: a) No official or individual is allowed to set the land price or determine the policy to benefit specific projects without authorization; b) no official or individual is allowed to decide the project undertaker, and the undertaker must be selected through public bidding, expert examination and collective decision-making so as to be open, fair and just; c) no official is allowed to gain interests with power for his relatives in land taken for development, household relocations and house demolitions.

Zhao: I'm very glad to see a new rising star among international China experts, since you have got a very deep understanding of China and offered a very professional view on China.

Doris: Thank you.

Zhao: Some people may think that Doris shares the glory of John, but I don't think so. Actually you are shining to each other like two stars. Two lights are certainly brighter than one. Do you agree? (To John)

John: Sure!

Doris: We have the good fortune to share interests. That way we can talk about everything at any time. We are truly nourishing each other.

Zhao: I've found that. Your new product is your new wisdom. Your " child " is wisdom; wisdom, more wisdom, and even more wisdom—a new book, another new book and another new book again.

John: Thank you very much for your generous and uplifting comments.

Zhao: Maybe you can celebrate your 15th or 20th anniversary of your marriage in China. Maybe we can ask the New World Press to design a Chinese style celebration for it.

John: It's a deal. We have just celebrated our 10th. That reminds me that recently I have read in *China Daily* that the cost for weddings, marriages and celebrations represents 10 percent of the GDP of China. Is that true?

Zhao: Ten percent means US $ 400 billion. Perhaps not that much! As far as I know, for those relatively rich families in China, they may spend RMB ¥ 100,000, that is, over US $ 10,000, on the wedding ceremony. I am going to check online to see how many young couples get married every year and how much money may be spent on their wedding ceremonies. ①

John: I mean if it's true, China is the most romantic country in the world. At least by these measures.

Filtering unhealthy "informative air"

Zhao: Maybe we should change our topic and talk about the contents of the Internet.

John: OK! The Internet plays a very important role in international communication. Information on the Internet brought pressure on traditional media, which were pressed to make more responsible reports of facts. I think TV is a big amplifier, whether it reports on China, Malaysia or the United States. For example, we just watched Michael Jackson's② funeral, which was amplified and brought distortion to reality.

---

① According to the data published by the Statistics Center for the Wedding Ceremony Industry of China, the total amount of consumption directly caused by marriages among city and township residents nationwide in 2009 exceeded RMB ¥ 600 billion with marriage registrations of 11.458 million newly married couples (http://www. Chinanews. com. cn/, March 6, 2010).

② A famous pop music singer who died unexpectedly on June 25, 2009 at the age of 50.

Doris: Communication on the Internet is not one-way; it is interactive. China is closing some of its channels for its people while opening its door to the world. Chinese may get a better understanding of the world through the Internet. We have seen that China has made great achievements since the reform and opening up, and lots of information channels were established. However, we found that some channels have been jammed or screened. For example, we couldn't log onto Facebook① today. Since the Chinese government opens its door to the world, why not give more freedom to the citizens for access to more information and comments, even criticism?

Zhao: Due to highly developed satellite TV and the Internet, the world has entered the Information Age. Some newly coined words emerged. One of them is "inforsphere," which may not be found in the dictionary. It means "informative air" with the combination of information with atmosphere. It can be put into something equivalent to "informative environment" in Chinese. Sometimes, the "informative air" is not clean enough and causes some problems when people inhale it. While the Internet produces a positive effect on society, some of its contents sometimes cause disorder in society, for example, some false or malicious information and pornographic information unhealthy to children. Therefore, we should be on the alert for it. Since the "informative air" sometimes contains unhealthy components that will cause chaos, we need to filter it.

John: I've heard the word years before. Actually what China is experiencing is what some Western countries have undergone. The key is who determines the legitimacy of the information. Citizens

---

① A social networking website launched online on February 4, 2004. It was originally designed for college students, but is now open to anyone 13 years of age or older. Its founder is Mark Zuckerberg, a former Harvard University student.

themselves or the government? In China, the answer is the government. That's a problem!

Doris: This is like a man sitting in a train with all its windows covered by a black curtain while being told that the outside view is not enjoyable. We do not like it.

Zhao: I immediately found that you are adept at metaphors. You are one of the smartest persons I've ever met. Is every Austrian as smart as you are?

Doris: (Laughing) Is every Chinese as smart and charming as you are?

Window glass with polarizing function

Zhao: (Laughing) Let me explain it. Actually the windows on the train are somewhat different, but not blocked. Otherwise, there would not be 384 million passengers[①] on it. I also use a metaphor to answer your question. The windows are made of glass with a function similar to polarization. To put it in a popular way, it can filter out some specific light to protect your eyes and enable you to leisurely observe the scenes outside the windows. The specific lights here are those lights unhealthy to society.

As far as I know, the routine management of Internet information is

---

① According to the data from the China Internet Network Information Center (CNNIC), there were already 384 million netizens in China as counted up to December 2009, and China has become No. 1 among users of the Internet in the world.

mainly in the charge of individual websites. There is a specific department in our government for Internet management. Of course, for those websites that make a lot of attacks on China, we do not welcome them.

John: Maybe we have different opinions about this.

Zhao: The Internet is no longer a virtual world isolated from the real world. It has already become an important part of society. So it is necessary to supervise the Internet according to the law. China has issued laws and regulations for the management of the Internet, including the Decision of the Standing Committee of the National People's Congress on the Maintenance of Internet Safety and the Regulation for the Management of Online Information Service enacted by the State Council, and relevant departments of the government have stipulated corresponding regulations. They should be observed by all Internet companies.

Part Five

Where Will China Go?

Creating a brand-new train

Zhao: We have discussed so many topics in the story of the development of China by sharing our experiences and exchanging our views. Now international media make a big fuss over the development model and the future of China. Of course, there is no consensus on the issue. Some call it "China at a crossroad," not knowing in which direction it is going.

John: After we have done all the research on China in the past years, we have, as said already, come to the conclusion that the world today has two models of development: the "Western Model" and the "China Model." You compared China to a train. I would say that China is creating a brand-new train that fits its demands and the demands of the 21st century very well. The West, on the other side, keeps repairing its 19th century train. China's new train might look better if it would pick up some of the traditional parts of the Western train, and the West would be well advised to have a look at China's train and learn from new technologies.

Zhao: Foreign media's comments on China, or international views on China, are diversified. Some make sense in the eyes of Chinese, while others are absurd. One of the absurd views is that a developed China will pose a threat to other countries. Another is that China will meet lots of difficulties; it cannot hold on; it will decline and collapse finally. This is an extreme view.

There are still some reasonable views, for example, a view that China's economic development and trade increase would bring opportunities to other countries' economic development. This may be concisely expressed as the "Opportunities Brought by China" view. Meanwhile, some people worry that China's exports have caused job losses in other countries. But they also should note that China's imports in large quantities have provided job opportunities in other countries. China will increase its domestic needs and strike a balance between imports and exports.

Some people say that China should take more international responsibilities while picking up its national strength. This is what we are doing. For example, in the U. N. peace-keeping missions, the number of personnel dispatched by China has greatly increased in recent years and it is more than that of any other permanent members of the U. N. Security Council. They have made very positive contributions to keeping local order, rescuing casualties in disaster-stricken areas and helping people to overcome difficulties in their lives. [1]

Doris: This is in accordance with China's strength and population.

John: In some areas, China's peace-keeping force is the largest in number.

Zhao: From those different comments, we can learn something very useful to us. Actually, the "China Model" was not put forward by China, nor does China intend to popularize the term. China has always held that policies should be formulated according to its own

---

[1] China became the 14th country to dispatch personnel to the U. N. peace-keeping troops in August 2009. It has sent soldiers, policemen and military observers on U. N. peace-keeping missions. China has exceeded any other permanent members of the U. N. Security Council in the number of dispatched personnel for peace-keeping tasks.

national conditions. It is doubtless that other developing countries should develop according to their own national conditions for success.

John: All China should do is go ahead! As for the "China Model," I believe it is deep-rooted in China and on its way to the future. In my view, in the near future China will make solid and sound steps because the "China model" wins the extensive support from the people and has made unprecedented success. So from a short-term or middle-term perspective, the "China model" and the Chinese people will both become increasingly mature. Of course, there is still a long way to run. As for China's future development, I can see a clear picture, because China has positioned its direction and is forging ahead at full speed.

Zhao: I believe most Chinese will appreciate your comments. China is not at a crossroad, but rather on its path to a harmonious society.

(To Doris, whose original specialty was performing arts) Our performing artist, do you think we should draw the curtain now?

Doris: Yes, perfect closing.

Praise for the Book

"It is obvious that China has already come to the center of the world stage. In order for people with different historical and cultural backgrounds in other countries to learn about China, recognize China, and better understand China, we must try our best to have talks on the same ground with people from other countries with different civilizations and foreign friends in different circles, and conduct friendly exchanges with them for more common understanding. In this sense, this book is a significant exploration, and I wish it a great success."

— Liu Binjie, Minister of the General Administration of Press and Publication of the People's Republic of China

"The great rise of the Chinese nation is one of the most influential world events today. Through a vivid and intelligent dialogue between Chinese and Western cultures, this book provides the readers with a new and unique perspective to observe and understand China today."

— Tie Ning, Chairwoman of the Chinese Writers' Association

"The cross-cultural interpretation and exchange as well as the philosophical thinking about the path taken by China in the past 30 years and the road ahead as shown in the dialogue between the three authors with different cultural backgrounds, discourse systems, and social experiences will offer readers rich inspiration and very valuable orientation to a more in-depth and comprehensive understanding of China."

— Zhou Mingwei, President of China International Publishing Group

"This is an honest dialogue between a couple in the field of futurism and an amiable Chinese official who dares to speak the truth. It is a prerequisite for China's adaptation to the world to have its story well told. The dialogue between these good storytellers has taught us some good methods: a) the necessity of being true; b) vividness without boredom; c) common concepts; d) human dignity; e) an outsider's perspective; f) no animosity. It is easy to tell a story, but it is not easy for others to give ear to it; and it is even less easy for the listener to take it seriously and respond to it. "

> — Liu Changle, Chairman of the Board of Directors and CEO of Phoenix TV

"The wise people who are rich in both political and life experiences have defined the 'China Model' in humorous expressions, vivid metaphors and glittering ideas. Mr. Zhao Qizheng would like to use the more appropriate expression the 'China Case,' which shows that China still needs to explore continuously on the way forward. This represents the common wish of many Chinese and will receive an extensive welcome from the outside world. "

> — Wang Jisi, President of International Relations Institute, Peking University

图书在版编目(CIP)数据

对话:中国模式 = The China Model: A Dialogue Between East and West:英文/赵启正,(美)奈斯比特,(奥)奈斯比特著;张洪斌,许靖国译. —北京:新世界出版社,2010.8
ISBN 978 - 7 - 5104 - 1085 - 7

Ⅰ.①对… Ⅱ.①赵… ②奈… ③奈… ④张… ⑤许… Ⅲ.①社会主义建设模式 – 研究 – 中国 – 英文②社会发展 – 研究 – 世界 – 英文 Ⅳ.①D616②D569

中国版本图书馆 CIP 数据核字(2010)第 117002 号

The China Model: A Dialogue Between East and West
对话:中国模式(英文版)

出 品 人:杨雨前
策　　划:吴　伟　张海鸥
作　　者:(中)赵启正　(美)约翰·奈斯比特　(奥)多丽丝·奈斯比特
翻　　译:张洪斌　许靖国
责任编辑:许靖国　李淑娟　葛文聪
英文审定:朱英璜
封面设计:贺玉婷
装帧设计:北京图腾视觉图文设计中心
责任印制:李一鸣　黄厚清
出版发行:新世界出版社
社　　址:北京市西城区百万庄大街24 号(100037)
总编室电话:+ 86 10 6899 5424　68326679(传真)
发行部电话:+ 86 10 6899 5968　68998705(传真)
本社中文网址:http://www.nwp.cn
本社英文网址:http://www.newworld – press.com
版权部电子信箱:frank@nwp.com.cn
版权部电话:+ 86 10 6899 6306
印　　刷:北京外文印刷厂
经　　销:新华书店
开　　本:787 × 1092　　1/16
字　　数:50 千字　　印张:9.75
版　　次:2010 年 8 月第 1 版　2010 年 8 月北京第 1 次印刷
书　　号:ISBN 978 - 7 - 5104 - 1085 - 7

定价:56.00 元